HOW TO READ AND UNDERSTAND
THE FINANCIAL NEWS

Also by Gerald Warfield

THE INVESTOR'S GUIDE TO STOCK QUOTATIONS
AND OTHER FINANCIAL LISTINGS

HOW TO BUY FOREIGN STOCKS AND BONDS

GERALD
WARFIELD

HOW
TO READ
AND
UNDERSTAND
THE
FINANCIAL
NEWS

Harper & Row, Publishers, New York
Grand Rapids, Philadelphia, St. Louis, San Francisco
London, Singapore, Sydney, Tokyo, Toronto

First PERENNIAL LIBRARY edition published 1988.

Designed by Ruth Bornschlegel

Library of Congress Cataloging-in-Publication Data
Warfield, Gerald.
　How to read and understand the financial news.

　"Perennial Library."
　Includes index.
　1. Journalism, Commercial—United States.
2. Finance—United States. I. Title.
PN4888.C59W37　1988　　332.63′2042　　86-45161
ISBN 0-06-091474-2 (pbk.)

92 MPC 10 9 8 7 6 5

*This book is dedicated to
my aunt,
Frankie Lee Slaton
of Fort Worth, Texas*

Contents

Acknowledgments

It is with gratitude that I acknowledge the individuals who assisted me in the writing of this book. In particular, I would like to thank Dr. Louis Fier of Brooklyn College and Stanton J. Lovenworth of Dewey, Ballantine, Bushby, Palmer & Wood for reviewing selected chapters. Also helpful was Joshua Hornick of Seward & Kissel.

Jon Clark reviewed many of the chapters for clarity and style. Martin Gonzalez also contributed in this area as he has so frequently done in the past.

Introduction

All of us routinely make financial decisions whether our background or training has prepared us to do so or not. Sometimes those decisions are relatively trivial, but sometimes they are once in a lifetime and have far-reaching consequences.

While it is always best to seek professional advice from qualified individuals (and it is not the purpose of this book to circumvent that step), the process of obtaining counsel or advice will be facilitated enormously by what you already know of current financial conditions. For example, just knowing how to read the stock tables and earnings reports will put you in a much better position to speak knowledgeably with a stockbroker and to evaluate his or her recommendations.

Having made the decision to learn about finance, you may wonder if you have sufficient time for it. Finance, after all, covers a lot of territory and includes some pretty formidable concepts. But this is not a college course in economics. It is a simple, commonsense approach that directly relates to your everyday experiences, and you'll be able to apply what you learn immediately.

The surprising thing is that the financial news, besides being informative, can also be an adventure—there is certainly no lack of heroes and villains. And while there are no easy answers, there are plenty of ways to make money, and there are relatively safe long-term goals that can be yours for the planning.

What we will do is start most chapters with news stories*: something like you might see in the headlines or hear on the evening news. We'll find out what the words mean and *don't*

---

*All right, so I made them up myself. But they are just like the articles and news stories you encounter every day. Also, I've used fictitious names, so don't rush out to buy any stock on the basis of these stories.

mean, what you can safely assume and what you'd better investigate more thoroughly.

In the financial news, even the simplest statement often tells us more than is obvious at first glance. Take the word "corporation" . . .

HOW TO READ AND UNDERSTAND
THE FINANCIAL NEWS

ONE

Is It a Corporation?

Look at the example on the following page. It may seem only to say that Trand's profits are up 22% (and no one needs to be told that that's good news). But wait: The word "corporation" was used and that tells us something important about Trand, particularly if you want to buy some of its stock.

Businesses in the United States usually take three principal forms: individual proprietorships, partnerships, and corporations.[1] We will get into the differences among these types a bit later, but for now we can say that of the three, incorporation is the most appropriate for a large business. This is because it offers a legal structure independent of the life or resources of a single individual. A corporation has a board of directors, the members and officers of which can be replaced. It also issues stock, so that when stock is available, ownership is easily transferable.

Assuming our example is from a newspaper, it is likely that Trand is a fairly large corporation and that it has many shareholders. However, it is possible that the company is "privately held," which means that the stock has never been offered publicly. Or the company could be "closely held," which means there may be a legal limit on the number of stockholders, and restrictions on the transferability of the shares.

Privately held and closely held corporations are not required to publish their financial reports, so frequently not much is known about them. A small number of investors may own all the shares, or it may be that members of only one or two families own the stock.

[1]Other forms are used less frequently. Typically, they are employed when there is some purpose other than the usual conducting of business. Some of the other forms are cooperatives, membership associations, trusts, and not-for-profit corporations.

Trand Corporation Profits Up 22%

CHICAGO—Trand Corp. reported profit gains in four of its five manufacturing divisions that resulted in a 22% overall increase from the previous year. . . .

Corporation: This tells us that Trand is a corporation as opposed to one of the other two principal forms under which business can be conducted in this country: as a partnership or as an individual proprietorship. The corporate structure offers the advantage of continuous existence (independent of the life of any one person) and limited liability for stockholders. The latter means that when the going gets rough, you can't lose any more than what you paid for the stock.

Dandor, Inc., To Purchase Beldon Manufacturing

NEW YORK—Dandor, Inc., announced today the acquisition of Beldon Manufacturing, a closely held company that . . .

Closely held: This is a corporation owned by a small number of stockholders, usually with legal restrictions on the transferability of its shares. "Privately held" means that the corporation's shares have never been publicly offered for sale. Neither type of corporation is required to publish an earnings or financial report. You might not be able to find out much about such companies.

Dallas Firm To Design Bronx Renovations

DALLAS—Smith, Mather & Dunn, the largest architectural firm in Dallas, has been awarded the contract for a 20-square block renovation project centered in . . .

Partnership: Many businesses such as architectural firms, law offices, accountants, etc., have been traditionally organized as partnerships. Although the word "partners" may not appear in the company name, it is usually assumed.

Blue Ridge Oil Co. To Form Limited Partnerships

LOS ANGELES—The Blue Ridge Oil Company has unveiled plans to offer limited partnerships as tax shelters to finance the drilling of 20 new oil and natural gas wells in Marlin County.

Limited partnership: This is a partnership in which there are two kinds of partners. Limited partners have no say in the running of the business and have limited liability similar to that of shareholders. General partners run the business and do have liability for the partnership debts. General partners are often corporations or other partnerships. Since all general partners are responsible for the debts of a partnership, this is a popular structure for tax shelters. Limited partners generally have no particular interest in the business; they have simply purchased an investment or a tax shelter.

Before going any further, let us now take a look at each of the three structures under which business can be conducted in the United States. This will give us some important perspectives from which to view corporations.

INDIVIDUAL OR SOLE PROPRIETORSHIP

This is a business that is completely owned and controlled by one person. In fact, legally, the owner *is* the business. Common examples are a small store or a doctor's practice. Among the advantages are that the owner has direct access to the profits and, in comparison to corporations, there are relatively few legal restrictions. There is also the advantage of one level of taxation; that is, only the proprietor is taxed, and not the business. The biggest problems are that it is difficult to obtain substantial long-term credit and that the owner has unlimited personal liability for all debts of the proprietorship.

From a bank's point of view, loans to proprietorships have certain risks. The existence of the business is dependent on one person; if that individual becomes disabled, retires, or dies, that is often (although not always) the end of the business. In addition, liability for the debts of the proprietorship extends to the personal property of the proprietor, and conversely, the business itself is subject to the owner's private debts. This is not very comforting to the proprietor or to the bank. For the proprietor, it means all personal property is at risk should the business fail; as far as the bank is concerned, personal collateral is often insufficient for the amounts of capital required by an ongoing business. There is also the risk that the proprietor's personal debts could adversely affect the business.

PARTNERSHIP

This is a business owned by two or more persons. Each partner in a regular partnership is essential to the continuous existence of the partnership. Each partner is liable for the business activities of the other within the partnership, and in most states this means unlimited and often unequal personal liability. Thus, if the assets of some partners are insufficient to meet claims on the partnership, other partners can be sued for additional amounts to make up for the shortfall.

The partners usually specify in their partnership agreement how much capital and effort is required from each partner and how profits are to be distributed. The death or departure of a partner will cause the partnership to dissolve and require reforming, unless continuity of the original name is one of the stipulations in the partnership agreement. Partnerships themselves are not taxed, but the income to the partners is taxed as ordinary income. A partnership's losses also pass on (called "flow through") to the partners, which is the reason the partnership format is chosen for tax shelters.

The partnership structure is appropriate for businesses where the individual contribution of each owner is crucial to the business (as is the case for architects), or where a certain amount of sharing of facilities can cut down on each partner's overhead (as is sometimes the case for dentists or accountants). In recent years there has been a tendency for businesses that traditionally form as partnerships to organize as corporations for certain tax advantages.

LIMITED PARTNERSHIP

A limited partnership is a special kind of partnership in that it has two kinds of partners: general partners and limited partners. The general partner (often there is only one and it may be a corporate entity or another partnership) runs the business, and bears unlimited liability. The limited partners (there are usually many) have no say in the business, even though they have contributed capital to the partnership. Since they are partners, they still have limited liability, but it is only to the extent of their investment. This feature has frequently been used in the formation of tax shelters.

As in our example, a drilling company may form limited partnerships for drilling new oil wells. The drilling company (or an affiliate created specifically for this purpose) will be the general partner, and investors (who need tax writeoffs as much as they need profits) will become limited partners by adding their capital to that of the general partner. With the pooled money, the general partner initiates the drilling.

Heavy startup costs are typical features of tax shelters, and the partnership will usually show losses the first few years. These losses can be written off by limited partners to the extent of their investment. By the time the wells begin producing, the limited partners have had a couple of years of tax writeoffs and now own part of a valuable business. They can then sell out or begin reaping their profits to the extent permitted by the partnership agreement. There are also strict securities laws that come into effect here too. At any rate, the limited partners will soon be looking for additional tax shelters to compensate for the new profitability of the present partnership. The general partner has profited by the tax writeoff too, but it has also been able to finance new drilling operations without bearing the entire startup costs alone.

CORPORATION

Most major businesses in the United States are organized as corporations. However, the flexibility of the corporate structure accommodates small businesses as well as the giants of industry. Do not assume that just because the word "corporation" appears in the name, a company is large.

ADVANTAGES

Many of the advantages of incorporation have already been mentioned, but perhaps the most significant are limited liability and the ability to raise large sums of capital.

Limited Liability. In the history of business and commerce the importance of limited liability can hardly be overestimated, because of the vast amounts of capital this concept has enabled businesses to raise. Basically, limited liability means that the owners of a business (in the case of corporations, the stockholders) have at risk only the capital which they have put into the enterprise (what they paid for the stock). If the business does well, the value of the percentage of the business owned by each investor increases accordingly; if the business does poorly, the value decreases accordingly.

With limited liability, the owner is protected in case the worst happens and the business fails. In this situation the business is often liquidated (all the assets sold), and if any capital is left over after paying the bills, it is divided among the owners according to their percentage of ownership. If after liquidation there are more debts than there is money to pay them, the owners will receive nothing; but even more important, the creditors do not have recourse to the investors for the obligations the corporation was unable to meet. Thus, while shareholders may lose their entire investment in a business, their losses are limited to the amount they put out for that investment. Shareholders cannot be sued for debts the company never paid. The ultimate losers in this situation are the creditors.

There have been cases where individuals have attempted to evade personal debts through the corporate structure and, more common, where corporate assets were interchangeable with personal assets. When this can be proved in court, the offending shareholder can then be sued for the debts of the corporation.

An interesting ramification of limited liability is the separation of ownership and management. If stockholders themselves had to manage the companies they owned, investors would probably be severely limited in the number of businesses in which they could invest. Instead, owners need only elect board members to be responsible for the business. The board supervises the corporation and elects the officers who run the operations. Shareholders also may vote on major issues that may come before the annual meeting. The officers and board of directors may, of course, own shares in the company and therefore also be owners (even majority holders), but that need not necessarily be the case.

Investors, whether individuals or institutions like banks or retirement funds, are free to own shares in a large variety of companies and thereby reduce the risk of their total investment by the diversity of their holdings. Each public company's management keeps its owners informed through periodic financial statements, such as those contained in annual and quarterly reports, and is usually accountable to the owners at the annual meetings or at other meetings called for special purposes.

Independence from One Person. If the president of a corporation retires or dies, another is elected to take his or her place. The business does not cease to exist or have to be reformed. If a shareholder sells his shares or dies, the ownership is simply transferred to a new purchaser or to an heir. Again, the business does not stop or have to be reformed. While this concept may seem obvious, it is far from arbitrary and is vital to maintaining continuity in a business and order in a marketplace. It is true, of course, that a company president can become strongly identified with the company, and his or her removal can be a blow to the company's prestige (not to mention its stock price). Nevertheless, the corporate structure is designed to minimize the negative effect of a change of management or ownership and to provide for smooth transitions in either of these instances.

DISADVANTAGES

Along with the advantages of incorporation, there are a few disadvantages. These include vastly increased paperwork and record-keeping, close regulation (particularly in some industries) by governmental bodies, and more taxes. It is the latter which is the most irksome to businesspeople and investors, and to explain it we must get ahead of ourselves a bit.

Double Taxation. Any money left after a company pays off its current creditors is profit. The business then has the option of putting all the profits back into the business, distributing all the profits to the owners, or a combination of the two.

Certain kinds of investment companies (that is, companies whose sole business is investing their capital in other companies) are required to divide up all their profits among their shareholders. This is the case with money funds, mutual funds, and closed-end investment companies. They are the exceptions with respect to distribution of profits, and since they will be explained in detail in a later chapter, no more will be said about them here.

Most businesses must have fresh infusions of cash in order to grow, to compete effectively in their markets, or even to maintain their present size or earning level. Equipment may have to be replaced, research may have to be financed, or new markets may need developing. Because of these requirements, it is usual for companies to keep the majority of their profits and to give a relatively small portion, if any, to the investors. Companies that grow rapidly will often plow all their profits back into the business, so that none is given to the shareholders (no dividends are paid at all). In such cases, the reward for the shareholders is the presumed increase in the value of the shares. Mature companies that expect relatively little growth, such as utility companies, may pay a relatively large portion of their profit back to their owners and are therefore characterized by relatively large dividends.

An important step, however, was omitted from this scenario. Before dividends are distributed from the profits, the profits are taxed. It is only after the government takes its share that stockholders receive dividends. But then, after dividends are in the hands of the investors, they are taxed again, as income to the taxpayer. This is called *double taxation.* Some corporations are able to shelter profits without paying taxes, but they are the exception rather than the rule.

Most businesspeople feel that to receive money which has already been subject to tax and then to be taxed on it again is unfair. Attempts to change the system, however, have proved futile so far. Other countries, by contrast, have rectified the situation to some degree by exempting paid-out dividends from corporate taxes, at least for certain industries or types of securities; only the profit retained by the company is taxed. Unfortunately, the United States has shown no inclination to follow suit, with the exception that taxpayers may exclude $100 ($200 in a joint return) on dividends received on U.S. stocks.

IS IT PUBLIC OR IS IT PRIVATE?

Before leaving the subject of corporate structure, we should clarify the concept of public ownership, because there are two different meanings of the word "public" in the financial news.

As mentioned earlier, a company whose shares are in the hands of a large number of shareholders is said to be publicly held. It is assumed that the ownership of such shares is freely transferable—for example, through purchase or sale of the shares on a stock exchange. To be listed on the New York Stock Exchange, companies must have over 2,000 shareholders. Generally, there are many more.

The first time a company offers its shares for sale to the general public, it is said to be "going public." Such a company may be newly formed, or it may be an existing company that had been privately held. After the initial offering of shares, any subsequent offering of a large block of shares by the same company is simply referred to as a "public offering."

Another use of the word "public" is to refer to the government. You see it in terms like "public debt" (which means the sum of all federal, state, and municipal debts), the "public sector"

Bendar Enterprises To Acquire Philo Corp.

PHOENIX—Bendar Enterprises, a small publicly held finance company, has announced plans to . . .

Publicly held: means that a corporation's stock is held by a relatively large number of investors and that generally the shares can be easily purchased or sold. Literally, it means there has been a public offering of its shares. It is the opposite of private or closely held.

Northgate, Inc., Announces Plans To Go Public

DETROIT—Northgate, a Cleveland-based toy manufacturer, announced plans for an initial public offering of two million shares next week. Northgate operates one factory in the Detroit area and . . .

"Going public": the first time that a company offers shares of its stock for sale to the general public.

Public offering: the sale of a large amount of new stock. If this is the first time the company has issued stock it is also known as an initial public offering. Generally, the marketing of such offerings is not handled by the company but by brokerage houses (underwriters) whose business it is to sell large stock offerings.

S.F. Electric Co. Asks 50% Rate Hike

OAKLAND—The San Francisco Electric Co., the largest public utility in California . . .

Public utilities: utility companies, whether or not they are publicly (government) or privately owned.

Publicly Owned Land To Be Auctioned

DENVER—Public land in Colorado, Texas, and New Mexico is to be . . .

Publicly owned: when used in contrast to privately owned, it means government ownership, whether at the local, state, or federal level.

Public Financing of Construction Outstrips Private Sector

LOS ANGELES—A study released today claims that construction spending in the public sector increased at a greater rate than . . .

Public financing: federal, state, or municipal financing either by the government bodies themselves or by the issuance of bonds.

Public sector: that portion of the economy controlled by federal, state, or local government spending (as opposed to the private sector).

(referring to that part of the economy composed of federal, state, and local government expenditures), and "public works" (government-sponsored buildings and projects). This is particularly confusing when the term is used to denote government ownership or government activities, as opposed to the private sector. For example, The Tennessee Valley Authority (TVA) is publicly (government) owned, in contrast to General Motors, which is privately owned.

Obviously, overlapping meanings of this kind can lead to ambiguity. Although the context will generally make the meaning clear, it is important to remember that the term "public" can have these two possible meanings.

Another usage that may cause problems is "public utility." Here the term refers to the public these utilities serve, not the owners; a public utility may be either publicly or privately owned. Most, in fact, are privately owned.

TWO

Stocks and Dividends

After the owners of a company vote to incorporate, all the equity (ownership) of the company becomes represented by its newly created stock. This is true whether the company is newly formed or whether it had a prior existence as a partnership or proprietorship. The owners decide how many shares to divide the company into, and they must then decide how many shares they will keep for themselves, how many (if any) they will award to others such as key employees, how many the corporation should retain as unissued shares (to be used at a later date), and how many to sell.

The capital the company raises by selling shares may be applied to all manner of business needs, such as expansion, development of products, and retirement of debt. It is through judicious use of this fresh infusion of cash that the company hopes to realize greater business potential.

Note that it is only when shares which are *owned by the company* are sold that the company itself gets any money. After an investor has purchased those shares, if they are subsequently sold to someone else, the *investor* selling the shares receives the money, not the company.

When investors buy and sell shares among themselves, they are said to be trading on the secondary market (the shares are not being offered by the company or a major stockholder for the first time). Stock exchanges are set up primarily to facilitate the trading of stocks on the secondary market, which constitutes the vast majority of all stock transactions.

Widget Company Plans Initial Offering

NEW YORK—Shareholders of the closely held Widget Company have voted to take the company public with an initial offering of 5 million shares of common stock. Making . . .

Palm Oil Industries Reduces Its Dividend

MIAMI—The board of Palm Oil Industries voted yesterday to slash its $2.00 dividend to $1.75. The first quarter payment, scheduled to be distributed the 15th of next month . . .

Marlin Industries Gets Approval for Preferred Issue.

CHICAGO—Shareholders of Marlin Industries approved a plan yesterday to issue 2 million shares of preferred stock. The shares, which will be cumulative and nonvoting, will have a dividend of $1.50 per share making for a 5% return on the initial offering price. . . .

Pacific Shippers Creates New Class of Common

SEATTLE—Shareholders of Pacific Shippers, Inc., nervous about recent takeover attempts, have ratified a company plan to create a class B common stock with ten times the voting power of the ordinary common. The plan calls for the one million shares to be . . .

Common stock: a unit of ownership in a corporation. Corporations sell these units to raise capital. Stockholders receive dividends, if they are distributed, as well as annual reports, and they have a claim to the assets of the company in case of liquidation. "Shares," incidentally, is just another word for "stocks."

Dividend: a distribution of some of the profits of the company to the owners—the shareholders. Dividends are usually stated as an annual per share figure, with one-fourth that amount paid every three months. Be careful that you know which is being referred to. In this example, the dollar amounts refer to the annual figure.

Preferred stock: similar to common stock, except that it usually does not have voting privileges and, more important, usually has a dividend rate that is fixed (in this way, it is similar to bonds). This dividend is usually more secure than the dividend of common shares because it is paid first. Sometimes it is cumulative, and sometimes it is secured by assets of the company.

Cumulative: the *dividend* is cumulative. That is, if the dividend is missed for one or more years because the company couldn't afford it, the obligation to pay holds over from year to year. Making up missed cumulative preferred dividends takes precedent over current common stock dividends.

Class A, class B: sometimes a company will issue more than one type of common or preferred stock. The issues will be distinguished by the labels "class A," "class B," and so on. Usual differences among separate issues of common stock concern voting privileges, for example, each class B share may get 10 votes for every one share of stock. (Currently this is not permitted on the New York Stock Exchange.) Differences between classes of preferred stock usually have to do with the dividend rate, voting privileges, whether they are cumulative or noncumulative, and priority of claim on assets of the corporation.

COMMON STOCK

There are two major types of stock: common stock, which a corporation must always issue, and preferred stock, whose issuance is optional. Preferred stock, which we will discuss later, is a kind of hybrid between stocks and bonds and is not issued nearly as frequently as common.

ADVANTAGES

Stock brings with it a number of advantages:

Transferability. One of the foremost advantages of stock is the ease with which ownership can be transferred.[1] If the market value of your stock goes up, you can usually sell immediately for a profit. Likewise, if it starts to slide, you can also sell immediately, thereby cutting your losses. Under almost any circumstances you can convert your investment into cash without delay. This may not sound like a major advantage at first, but if the transfer of stocks were as involved, and took as much time, as the transfer of titles in real estate, then the movement of stocks on financial markets would be seriously impeded.

Being able to buy and sell stocks quickly, and having an adequate supply of buyers and sellers on hand to accommodate any and all orders, makes for a condition in financial markets which is called "liquidity." Stock markets in the United States and all over the world provide liquidity for securities by bringing buyers and sellers together.

Sometimes stock in a small or highly speculative company does not enjoy liquidity. It may be that only a few brokers carry an inventory of the stock, that there are relatively few stockholders, or that little is known about the company. In this case, shareholders may have a hard time finding buyers when they want to sell, particularly if the price is falling. Such stocks are said to be thinly traded.

The term "deep" market relates to the liquidity of a stock, although depth specifically refers to the ability of a market to

[1]This is true of all stocks traded on stock exchanges, where they come under the regulation of the exchanges and of the Securities and Exchange Commission. You will rarely encounter any other kind of stock, but there are some shares, such as those of a closely held corporation, which can be very difficult to transfer.

absorb large buy or sell orders without unduly affecting the price of the security.

Dividends. An important benefit of stock ownership is the possibility of receiving dividends. Dividends are usually declared on an annual per share basis but paid quarterly. Thus, from a stock with a $1 dividend, you will receive 25 cents per share every three months. When reading about dividends in the news, be careful to determine whether the reference is to the yearly total or a quarterly payment.

Important as dividends are, they are not usually high enough to be the sole reason for buying a particular stock. You would usually receive more money from interest on bonds of a similar quality. But with stock you have a greater likelihood of capital gain by eventually selling the stock for more than you paid for it. Capital gains are also taxed at a lower rate than dividends.

As mentioned in the previous chapter, not all corporations decide to distribute dividends to shareholders. Of those that do, occasionally *shares,* or a combination of shares and cash, may be given as a dividend. (There was even a recent case where a mining company paid its dividend in silver.) When a stock's dividend is small or nonexistent, the sole reason for buying the stock is to hope for capital gains.

Voting. Most common stock carries with it the privilege of voting. You may vote for members of the board of directors or help decide important issues such as increasing the number of shares. The voting privilege is a result of the fact that shareholders are owners. As an owner, you are entitled to make decisions about how the company should be run or at least to appoint those (the board of directors) who will make such decisions for you.

The company or your broker will mail you a form in advance of the annual meeting requesting your vote or the assignment of your proxy so that someone whom you designate can vote your shares. Frequently, investors accept the recommendations of management on all items and are willing to vote a blanket "yes" or to give their proxy to the corporate secretary so their shares can be voted in the way the board thinks best. These choices will be clear to you on the form you receive.

Individual shareholders do not generally regard voting as a significant aspect of owning shares. While you may not feel that your 100 shares of XY&Z will count for much when you vote them in a corporate election, the principle is nevertheless important. When shareholders are well organized, they can sometimes have an effect at annual meetings and influence the policies of the company. When a group of shareholders controls the majority of votes in a corporation, they can do anything they please (within the limitations of the certificate of incorporation, which also can be changed), including replacing members of the board of directors—even the president.

Shares of foreign companies available in this country are frequently nonvoting. This is because massive foreign purchases of a company's shares could effectively shift control of such a company outside its home country (foreigners could buy 51% of the shares). In order to have the advantage of marketing their shares internationally without running the risk of nonresident control, many foreign companies issue two classes of common shares, one voting and one nonvoting. The only type available to nonresidents is the nonvoting kind.

Annual Report. Another benefit of stock ownership includes receipt of current financial data as a part of annual and quarterly reports. Many investors base their investment decisions on figures from annual reports, so they are quite important. Since Chapter Five will be devoted to annual reports nothing more will be said about them here.

Claim to Assets. As with any owner, a stockholder has a claim to the assets of the company. Should the company liquidate, the money would be used first to pay creditors and second to be distributed to owners according to their percentage of ownership. In general, the hierarchy of payments would be: bondholders first (bonds are actually loans, so bondholders are creditors), preferred stockholders second, and common stockholders last.

Within these categories there may be some issues whose claims to assets are prior to others. For instance, it may be that one corporation has two issues of preferred stock, so that the claims of a preferred B issue may take precedent over the claim of a preferred A issue. A security whose claims to assets takes precedence over another is said to be a "senior" issue.

Since it was mentioned in the previous paragraph, it should be noted that there are sometimes different classes of both common and preferred stock (class A, class B, and so on). These may be distinguished by a different number of votes per share, a different dividend, or prior claims to the assets of the company in case of liquidation.

Subscription Privileges. If a company issues new shares, it will frequently make them available first to present stockholders, sometimes at a reduced price. This is called a "subscription privilege." Should you be eligible for such an offer, you or your broker will be notified directly by the company. Usually there is a limit on the number of shares you can acquire in this fashion, such as one share for every two you currently own.

PREFERRED STOCK

Preferred stock is usually distinguished by a higher dividend than the common shares of the same company, and often this dividend is more secure than the dividend of common shares. For instance, the board of directors decides on the common share dividend from year to year, depending on how well the company is doing. But for preferred stock, there is a stated dividend rate which the corporation must meet each year (assuming there is sufficient profit to cover it). In this sense, the claim to dividends of preferred stock is prior to the claim of common stock. If there is *only* enough profits to meet the preferred dividend, then the common stockholders will go without.

Sometimes the dividend of preferred stock is cumulative, which means that if there are insufficient funds to pay it one year the obligation holds (is cumulative) through subsequent years. Meeting this back obligation takes precedence over the distribution of dividends to common shares.

One would think that with a relatively high dividend guaranteed, preferred stock would be more popular than common stock. However, preferred stock does not share the potential for appreciation in market value that common stock does. When significant news is heard about a company, the price of the common will react more strongly than the price of the preferred. It is probably the unchanging dividend of preferred stock that keeps its price more stable than that of common.

Even if a company does well, the preferred dividend usually remains the same. This may contribute to the fact that the market price of preferred stock is not as volatile as that of common. The point of acquiring preferred shares is usually to establish a relatively safe, long-term, income-producing investment. The turnover of preferred shares is not nearly as high as that of common shares.

CONVERTIBILITY

Preferred shares are sometimes convertible, which means that they may be exchanged for a fixed number of shares of common stock. Whether it is profitable for the investor to do so depends on the market price of the common shares and the conversion rate (2 for 1, 3 for 1, and so on). One does not usually need to go to the trouble of converting preferred into common, because the conversion value will be reflected in the market price of the preferred shares. Convertibility links the market price of the preferred stock to the market price for the common and can cause the price of a preferred issue to be just as volatile as that of the common.

Let's take an example: You buy a convertible preferred issue at $25 per share. It may be converted at any time into 5 shares of common stock. When you made your purchase the common shares were selling at $4 per share, so there was no reason to consider conversion (5 × $4 = $20). You may have selected the preferred shares simply because of their high dividend.

A year later, the price of the common has gone up to $7 per share. Now if you convert, the 5 common shares will be worth $35, $10 more than the per share price of the preferred shares. However, you may not need to make the conversion, because at the point where the value of the converted common overtakes the current market value of the preferred shares (this is called "conversion parity"), the price of the preferred will begin to track the common shares (one preferred share will approximate the market price of five common shares). The ratio wouldn't be exactly 1 to 5, however, because the market would take into consideration the high dividend of the preferred shares, which the common presumably wouldn't have.

OTHER IMPORTANT CONCEPTS

OVERSUBSCRIBED

When any offering of stock is made available to the public for the first time, brokers take orders for the new stock before it is actually issued. Sometimes this leads to more orders for the stock than there are shares to go around. When this happens to an issue, it is said to be oversubscribed. Small orders will usually still be filled, but large orders are accommodated on a pro rata basis (all orders will be reduced by an equal percentage if there is an insufficient number of shares to go around).

Later, when the security finally comes out, it will experience an immediate increase in price. This is a classic case of the pressures of supply and demand. There is more demand than supply, so the price goes up. When this happens during an initial offering, brokers call it a "hot" issue.

STOCK SPLITS

Sometimes companies decide to change the number of shares outstanding by means of a "stock split." A 2 for 1 split, for instance, would immediately double the total number of shares, and the dividend would be cut in half. The immediate value of the new stock would generally be exactly half that of the old.

A possible reason for such a move would be to reduce the market price of the stock. Some companies might feel that their shares had risen to such a high price that it limited the purchase of those shares to wealthy and institutional investors. Brokers have noticed that some U.S. investors have an aversion to purchasing odd lots. (One hundred shares is the usual round lot; anything less is an odd lot.) One of the ways to make shares more affordable is to reduce the per share price by means of a stock split and thereby lower the total cost of a round lot.

Although technically the new stock created by a split should be valued at exactly the ratio of the split, such a move by a corporation is often interpreted as a sign of strength. If a stock split is followed by increased investor demand, there may be some increase in the market price of the new stock.

"Reverse splits" are also possible. This might happen, for instance, if a penny stock (shares selling for less than a dollar) were to be doing well and the company wanted to improve its image. U.S. investors are often suspicious of shares that are cheaply priced, so a reverse split would increase the per share cost to a level at which the typical U.S. investor would be comfortable. A 1 for 10 reverse split would, for instance, change the price of a 50 cent stock to $5.

It should be noted that many foreign markets do not necessar-

Investors Flock to Convert Shares

COLUMBUS—Investors holding Southern United's class C convertible preferred shares have until Friday to convert each of their preferred shares into 10 shares of the company's common stock. The October 1 deadline has caught many investors. . . .

Convertible: one security can be exchanged for another, usually of a different type. Many preferred shares are convertible into common shares of the same company at a fixed rate of conversion (10 shares of common for 1 of preferred). The price of the convertible will not usually fall below that of the total value of the securities into which it can be converted.

Winger To Split Stock

BOSTON—Winger Bubble Gum, Inc., has announced a 2 for 1 stock split effective June 1. The new stock will bring Winger's shares outstanding to 40 million. . . .

Stock split: Corporations may decide to split their existing stock at any ratio desirable (two shares for one, five shares for three). Although generally interpreted as a sign of strength, the market price of new shares is initially pegged at the ratio of the split. Thus a 2 for 1 split would make the new shares worth half the value of the old. Reverse splits are also possible.

Monolith Computers Initial Offering Oversubscribed

PHILADELPHIA—A spokesman for Monolith Computers reported yesterday that its initial offering of 10 million common shares was heavily oversubscribed. He assured investors, however, that small orders for 500 shares or less would be . . .

Oversubscribed: When there are more purchasers requesting shares of an initial or subsequent public offering than there are shares to go around, the issue is said to be oversubscribed. This usually causes the price of the security to go up as soon as it begins trading on the secondary market.

ily share this prejudice. Some of the bluest of blue chip stocks on the Tokyo Stock Exchange sell for around a dollar a share. And this in no way reflects on the quality or degree of speculativeness of the stock.

THREE

How They Make Stock—And Sell It

Companies are incorporated under state law. While regulations are relatively uniform from state to state, there are a few differences[1] that make it more desirable to incorporate in some states than in others. In addition, some of the more popular states, like Delaware, don't require that business be conducted within their state so long as the corporation maintains a mailing address within the state and retains an agent for serving legal papers.

THE CREATION OF AUTHORIZED STOCK

When a company incorporates, the certificate of incorporation is approved by the state secretary and then, in most states, is filed with the clerk of the relevant county. One of the provisions in the certificate is the number of shares that will represent the corporation; these shares constitute the total of all "authorized stock."

If, for example, the corporation is to be owned equally by two people and it is never expected that additional shares will be needed for sale to other parties, the number of shares can be as small as two—one for each owner.

The value of the shares will be partly dependent on how many

---

[1] Such as latitude for management, reporting requirements, shareholders' rights, and permissibility of takeover defenses.

Buffalo Power Tools To Market 10 Million New Shares

BUFFALO—A company spokesman for Buffalo Power Tools said that shareholders had ratified 10 million new shares, bringing the company's total of authorized shares to 40 million. However, 5 million of the new shares will remain unissued, bringing the total of shares outstanding to 35 million. . . .

Authorized stock: the total number of shares stated in a company's certificate of incorporation. This number of shares represents the total of the company's capital and cannot be increased without a vote of the shareholders. Even so, the company can elect not to issue all of its stock.

Shares outstanding: all shares issued by the company, not counting any treasury stock that may be held by the company.

Blended Foods To Offer 3 Million Shares

BALTIMORE—The Blended Foods board of directors said today that the company will sell half of its treasury stock, or 3 million shares. This is the first . . .

Treasury stock: shares originally issued by the corporation but since reacquired on the secondary market. When a corporation purchases its own shares, they become treasury stock and are treated for most purposes like unissued shares.

Brown Family Sells Shares of Atlantic Tide

ATLANTA—A spokesperson for the Brown family of Atlanta, Georgia, said yesterday that half of the family's holdings in Atlantic Tide would be sold. The 4 million shares would constitute the largest block of Atlantic Tide stock to come to the market since the initial offering two years ago. The sale will be handled by a consortium of five investment bankers, but the spokesperson declined to name the firms.

Block: a large number of shares which, because of its size, is usually purchasable only by institutional investors.

Investment bank: a kind of security broker that helps to sell shares of an initial or secondary offering. A group of investment bankers or underwriters that share responsibility for handling a primary issue or secondary offering is called a syndicate.

shares are created. One of only two shares representing a company will be worth more than one of one million shares representing the same company. But no matter what the initial number, more shares can be created only after a vote of the shareholders. If there were no restriction on the number of shares a corporation could issue, then it could continuously devalue, or "dilute," the stock already issued by issuing more and more new shares. This kind of "printing press" approach to issuing stock could ultimately destroy the value of a company's shares.

ISSUED AND UNISSUED SHARES

A corporation generally divides its initially authorized shares into two major groups. Both the shares offered for sale to the public and those paid out to individuals (often board members) in recognition of their initial investment or service become *issued* stock (also called "issued and outstanding"). Those shares retained by the corporation—given to no one, not even board members—become *unissued stock.*

Board members and other parties that receive large initial blocks of shares often hold them for a long time, hoping that the company's progress will bring increases in investor demand, causing their shares to appreciate in value. These large blocks of shares may not be actively traded among the public for a long time. On the other hand, many of the shares which are made available to the public and are purchased in the initial offering will start trading right away on the secondary market. These shares may pass through the hands of hundreds of investors over the years.

There is a variety of things that the corporation can do with its unissued shares. It may hold them in reserve, hoping to raise capital by selling them at a later date. It may eventually distribute them to current shareholders in the form of stock dividends. This can be a painless way of meeting dividend expectations, particularly when a company is short of cash. Along these same lines, the unissued shares could also be awarded as bonuses to officers or employees. Another interesting use could be as payment for the purchase of the shares of other companies. This might happen in the course of a takeover attempt, of expansion or diversification of the company's business, or simply as a prudent investment.

So long as stock held by a company remains unissued, it possesses none of the ordinary benefits of stock; it has no voting rights and pays no dividends.

TREASURY STOCK

Sometimes a company will buy back its own stock on the open market. For instance, if the price of a company's shares falls below a certain point, the corporate treasurer might feel that the bargain price constitutes a good investment for the company, and purchases at that time would provide price support for the stock. After all, who would be in a better position to decide whether the shares were a good investment at the price?

There is another advantage to a corporation purchasing its own stock: It increases the intrinsic value of the shares that remain issued and outstanding. We will get into the specifics of that situation in Chapter Five.

Shares reacquired by a company become what is called "treasury stock." Treasury stock can be used for any of the purposes mentioned above for unissued stock. In addition, it can later be sold in the marketplace after the price has risen, thus making a profit for the company. Note that it is not the full price received that constitutes the profit, but only the difference between the purchase price and the sale price, just as with ordinary investment transactions.

Shares that become treasury stock do not earn dividends. Such shares also lose their voting rights. This prevents unscrupulous directors from using corporate money to buy shares and, with the votes of these shares, controlling the company.

To recapitulate briefly, all stock created by the corporate charter becomes authorized stock. Stock retained by the corporation is unissued stock. Stock sold to the public or given to the original investors becomes issued and outstanding. Stock that was originally issued, but which has subsequently been reacquired by the corporation, becomes treasury stock.

SELLING STOCK

SECONDARY OFFERING

After a corporation has already gone public, any sale of a large block of shares not owned by the issuing corporation is called a "secondary offering" or a "secondary distribution." The term refers to the fact that the sale would normally be made on the secondary market. However, the amount of shares offered in this manner is generally too large to be accommodated in the ordinary course of securities trading, so the actual transaction may be handled by one or more brokerage firms.

INVESTMENT BANKING

You will occasionally see references in the financial news to an "investment banker" or "investment banking." This has nothing to do with banking in the usual sense of savings deposits, checking accounts, or loans. Investment bankers are underwriters. They help companies "go public" by handling the sale of the initial offering of stock, or by marketing newly created issues of stock from a company that has already gone public. They also arrange mergers and acquisitions.

Investment banking is a subject worthy of an entire book in itself, and we will not go into the intricacies here. Basically, the investment banker, or underwriter, brings together the issuing company and the investing public.

Investment bankers often are also brokerage houses. When a large company goes public, an entire group of broker/investment bankers (underwriters) assume responsibility for selling (underwriting) the new shares. The group of underwriters working on a single stock issue is called a "syndicate."

When a consortium brings a corporation public, the initial offering is often announced in newspapers, especially financial papers like the *Wall Street Journal,* in ads called "tombstones." The term in no way reflects on the mortality of corporations, but instead suggests the heavy, engraved-like quality of the main type and the heavy border surrounding the ad.

STOCK EXCHANGES

Stock exchanges are usually defined as places where buyers and sellers of securities are brought together for the purpose of executing transactions. It would be more correct to say that they are places where the *agents* of buyers and sellers come together, since stock exchanges are the exclusive domain of stockbrokers. Perhaps even more important than the exchange's role in bringing the brokers physically together is the multitude of sophisticated support facilities that the exchange offers. The New York Stock Exchange could never handle its enormous volume of transactions for instance, without all the computers, reporting, communications staff, and equipment that it offers.

Stock exchanges are mentioned often in the financial news because most of the nation's major securities usually trade on

① Standard disclaimer stating that this notice is not an offer to sell stock. Such offers can legally be made only through a prospectus (see item 8 below). In principle, tombstones are only for information purposes; often the stock has already been sold out.

② New issue means this is an initial offering. The security is being sold by the company through the underwriters (investment bankers) listed at the bottom of the ad. The company will receive only the net proceeds of the sale.

③ This is the effective date—the first date on which the offering may commence. It is often the same date the ad is placed.

④ This is only the total number of shares being offered for sale (issued). There may have been many more authorized by the corporation's charter, but the board of directors has decided not to issue them.

(5) Preferred shares and bonds are also offered in tombstone announcements. Sometimes you will see units offered which will consist of, for example, 1 share and 2 warrants. (The warrant is like an option—see Chapter Twelve—and can be used in the future to purchase more shares at a specified price after a specified date.)

(6) The par value of a common stock is an almost meaningless value, being an amount assigned to the stock at issue solely for bookkeeping purposes (see Chapter Five). Many common stocks are issued without having been assigned a par value, as is the case here. Par value *is* important for preferred issues, since sometimes the dividend is stated as a percent of par value. For bonds, the par value is the face amount (see Chapter Nine).

(7) This is the price at which the security will sell (or has been sold) in advance of its issuance. After issue, demand on the secondary market will determine the price, as is the case for all outstanding securities. If there are more offers to buy than there are shares to go around in the initial offering, the stock is called a "hot issue," and the market price will rise as soon as the shares begin trading on the secondary market. Incidentally, shares of a new issue cannot be purchased "on margin," a type of credit you can get from your broker using other shares you own as collateral. The shares must be paid for in full by the purchaser.

(8) No legal sale of a new issue can be made without the buyer receiving a prospectus in advance of the transaction. In fact, if you don't receive a prospectus before you receive a confirmation notice of the trade, you have a legal right to cancel the transaction without penalty within a reasonable amount of time. Since new issues are generally more speculative than securities already trading on the open market, the prospectus requirement prevents a broker from strongarming you into buying a security over the phone about which you may know very little.

There are two prospectuses. The preliminary prospectus is called a "red herring" because of a statement printed on the cover in red to the effect that the registration hasn't been declared effective by the Securities and Exchange Commission. The purpose of the preliminary prospectus is to stimulate sales when the registration is first filed with the SEC. The SEC may or may not require revision or emendations. After the SEC has accepted the preliminary prospectus a new prospectus, without the red lettering, is printed and used for offering the shares. The reference in the tombstone ad is to the second prospectus.

(9) The mention "lawfully offer these securities in such state" refers to the fact that all offerings must be cleared for purchase in every state in which they are being sold (this is called "blue-skying" the issue). In some states the process is fairly automatic. Most major offerings will be cleared for sale in all states. Also, the brokerage firm itself must be registered to sell new issues in your particular state. If you call a broker with whom you don't have an account to inquire about a new issue, one of the first things he or she will ask you is what state you live in.

(10) This is the list of investment bankers or underwriters that make up the syndicate bringing out the issue. Those with the largest numbers of shares to sell are listed first, and in bolder type than those with a relatively minor stake. If you wish to acquire the security at the initial price, before it starts trading on the secondary market, you must get the shares through one of these firms or a firm specifically contracted by one of them to sell the securities. Some will be retail brokers, selling to the general public, but some may handle only sales to large institutional buyers.

stock exchanges, and much that is newsworthy about a company is reflected in the large volume of purchases and sales of its stock made in this marketplace. Since they are centers for large numbers of transactions, overall trends can often be spotted on exchanges, and a record of these transactions constitutes a measurable profile of investor sentiment concerning specific securities or the market in general.

If a company wishes to have its stock traded on an exchange (this is called being "listed" on an exchange), it must apply to the relevant exchange, meet certain specified requirements, and pay fees. The requirements for listing on the New York Stock Exchange are a minimum of $2.5 million in pretax earnings a year, a minimum of 1 million shares in public hands, net assets of $16 million, and at least 2,000 shareholders of a minimum of 100 shares each.

An issue may be delisted—removed from trading on an exchange—if it falls below any of the above requirements. Also, if a corporation is acquired by another corporation, its shares may cease to trade independently of its new owner. The new owner, for instance, might issue more of its own shares to replace those of the acquired corporation.

After a security is listed on the New York or American Stock Exchange, all transactions on the floor of the exchange involving that security must go through a specialist assigned to that security. All trading therefore takes place at this one spot, and the trader is responsible for keeping an orderly market in that security. To maintain this "orderly market," the specialist may enter into trades himself, buying and selling for his own account in order to balance the supply and demand for the stock. While the prices of stocks can change from minute to minute, it is the job of the specialist to see that prices do not swing back and forth erratically because of momentary imbalances of buy and sell orders.

Both the New York Stock Exchange and the American Stock Exchange make use of specialists. Specialists are not employees of the companies whose stocks they trade; new stock listed on an exchange may simply have a specialist assigned to it. But sometimes the choice of the particular individual is subject to a certain amount of negotiation. Large, actively traded issues may require the assignment of several specialists.

At various times, the specialist system has come under attack. Among the criticisms leveled are that specialists have a monopoly on securities trading, that they have more power than a free market system calls for, and that many are undercapitalized and therefore unable to keep an orderly market in a time of crisis. For better or for worse, you will probably see references to stock specialists in the financial news for a long time to come.

THE OVER-THE-COUNTER (OTC) MARKET

The primary over-the-counter (OTC) market is known as NASDAQ. It brings buyers and sellers together too, but not physically. Instead of a huge place, like an exchange, the NASDAQ system offers a computer and telephone communication network that efficiently connects buyers and sellers all over the country. (To be literally correct, we would have to say that again, like exchanges, NASDAQ brings together the *brokers* of buyers and sellers.)

The term "over-the-counter" refers back to times when such securities, because they were not accepted for listing on a stock exchange, had to be purchased at the offices of brokers or banks —literally over the counter.

The NASDAQ system is so efficient now that it has begun to rival the New York Stock Exchange in importance, and many major companies sell their securities over-the-counter out of choice, and not because they cannot get listed on the New York or American Stock Exchange. More will be said about the NASDAQ system in Chapter Four.

FOUR

Reading the Stock Tables

Financial tables are found in the business section of most newspapers. In these lists are current market prices ("quotations") for a wide variety of investment instruments. Small papers may carry only stock quotations, while larger papers will include quotations for bonds, options, government securities, commodities, and financial futures. In this chapter we will concern ourselves only with stock quotations.

Stock quotations fall into two broad categories: quotations for those shares that are traded on exchanges, and quotations for those that are traded over-the-counter. Although the differences between them are not as great as they once were, it is still useful to understand the distinctions that do exist.

EXCHANGE-TRADED STOCKS

Many people think of a stock exchange as a place where only stocks are traded. Stock exchanges, however, routinely handle bonds, as well as warrants, options, and even financial futures. All these instruments will be examined in the following chapters. For now, the point is that while all may be traded on stock exchanges, the volume of shares traded is usually greater than all the rest. For example, on the New York Stock Exchange, even though there are 3,750 bonds listed, their dollar volume doesn't begin to approach that of the 2,300 stock issues.

Trading on a stock exchange may be done only by brokers (including specialists, as described in Chapter Three) who have a "seat" on the exchange; that is, they have paid a membership fee and been accepted as responsible members of the investment community by the governing board of the exchange. They are also bound by strict rules concerning the manner in which trading must take place.

In the United States, when we speak of exchanges we usually mean the New York Stock Exchange (NYSE), the largest stock exchange in the world, and the American Stock Exchange (AMEX), which is the second-largest exchange in the country. Although the comments that follow refer specifically to those two

| 52-Week | | | | Yld. | PE | Sales | | | | |
High	Low	Stock	Div.	%	Ratio	100s	High	Low	Last	Chg.
32⅞	20	Ickerd	1.04	3.5	14	903	30⅛	29¾	29¾	−⅛
38¼	31	IdisBr	1.60	5.0	12	231	32¼	32	32½	−¼
18⅝	13¾	IDO	.28	1.7	13	283	16½	16⅜	16½	+½
34¼	19⅞	Idora	.80	2.5	15	72	32¼	31⅞	32⅛	−⅛

① **The highest and lowest prices** paid for the stock during the last twelve months. The price is in dollars per share, so that 32⅞ = $32.875. One hundred shares, called a round lot, would cost $3,287.50.

② **Abbreviated name** of the company issuing the stock. Note that the names are alphabetized by the words for which the abbreviations stand, rather than the letters in the abbreviation. Therefore, the alphabetization will frequently be out of order according to the letters you see.[1]

③ **The dividend** is the annual per share amount that stockholders may expect to receive. Dividends are usually paid quarterly (every three months), so each payment will be one-fourth the amount shown.

④ **Yield** is the current annual dividend represented as a percent of the current price of the stock. This percent reflects the expected rate of return on the stock if bought at the current price. If you bought your shares at another price or years ago when a different dividend was being paid, the yield on your investment is different from the current yield.

⑤ **PE Ratio** (see Chapter Twelve) is the current per share price divided by the current annual earnings per share.

⑥ **Sales** show the number of round lots (100 shares each) that changed hands for the time period covered by the quotations.

[1] The Investor's Guide to Stock Quotations, by the author, lists all the abbreviations of listed and NASDAQ OTC stocks. (Published by Harper & Row.)

exchanges, it should be pointed out that the United States has five other stock exchanges: the Pacific Stock Exchange (which has two floors, one in Los Angeles and one in San Francisco), the Midwest Stock Exchange (located in Chicago), the Philadelphia Stock Exchange, the Boston Stock Exchange, and the Cincinnati Stock Exchange. While each of these five smaller exchanges has some exclusive stocks (usually issues of small or locally owned companies), they also deal in stocks that are traded on the NYSE or on the AMEX. Such stocks are said to be "dually listed." No stocks, however, are traded on both the NYSE and the AMEX.

Although these exchanges (collectively called "regional exchanges") are much smaller than the NYSE or AMEX, they have some distinct advantages. Since there is no extra charge for odd-lot transactions (sales or purchases of less than a hundred shares) on the Midwest exchange, odd-lot orders for NYSE-listed stocks are frequently transferred to Chicago for execution (assuming that the stock is also listed there). On the Pacific exchange, trading in stock dually listed on the NYSE continues after the NYSE has closed, since California is three time zones later than New York. The Philadelphia exchange has been particularly innovative in the development of option trading, including options on silver. The Cincinnati Stock Exchange is unique in that it has no trading floor; all transactions are completed via computer and telephone.

Trading on a stock exchange is usually described as a "two-way auction." A two-way auction is not like the usual auction, where two or more buyers actively bid against one another for the privilege of purchasing a single object from a passive seller, thereby driving the eventual sale price in one direction—higher. It is, instead, an auction where both buyers and sellers are actively bidding against one another. The sellers want the highest prices possible, and the buyers want the lowest prices possible, thereby pulling stock prices in both directions.

This describes an ideal market situation. However, on the New York Stock Exchange, face-to-face trading between buying and selling brokers happens only for relatively large orders, usually involving 600 shares or more.

For less than 600 shares, the order to buy or to sell is routed to a computer located at the post where transactions in that specific security are usually handled by the specialist in that stock. Buy and sell orders are then matched up automatically as far as possible. While the two-way auction is thus electronically simulated, you cannot assume that an order for a few hundred shares of XYZ will see action on the floor of the exchange or that by itself the order has a chance of moving the price of the stock up or down.

QUOTATIONS FOR EXCHANGE-TRADED STOCKS

When the newspaper reports the market prices of stocks that are trading on exchanges, they report the last actual price at which the security changed hands. This is an important point to remember, because it is not always that way for stocks traded over-the-counter. Here is a typical quotation of a stock listed on the New York Stock Exchange.

As with all financial tables, keep an eye out for footnotes. Almost always indicated by a small letter, these notes tell you important information about a stock. Here are some footnotes used by the Associated Press that are referred to by letters appearing in the Div. (Dividend) column:

s = There has been a stock split (see Chapter Two) within the last 12 months. The price you see is the current price for the stock, and the 52-week high and low have been adjusted to reflect that split.

pf = This is a preferred issue of stock. Frequently, you will see the common share (no "pf") listed immediately above. Sometimes the same company will have several preferred share issues.

n = This is a new issue within the last 52 weeks, and the high and low prices shown reflect the range of prices since the start of trading.

Now let us proceed with the next items in the standard stock quotation. Some of the footnotes that might appear in the yield (Yld.) and Sales columns are these:

x = means the shares were traded ex-dividend yesterday (don't forget, today's paper reports on yesterday's market activity.) All holders of record (the official owners of stock) as of the day *before* yesterday will receive the upcoming dividend payment. If you bought the shares today, you will not receive this payment, but must wait until the next dividend payment, usually three months away. All other things being equal, the stock should sell for less today than it did yesterday.

z = means sales in full. The number in the sales column is the actual number of shares sold, not the number of hundred-share round lots. This is usually indicated only for very high-priced preferred stocks that frequently trade in odd lots.

The next columns of the quotation are prices. The high and low are the highest and lowest prices actually paid for shares of the stock during the period covered by the quotation. If you are reading a Sunday newspaper, or a weekly like *Barron's,* the period covered by the quotation might be the entire previous week. If you are reading a daily paper, the prices shown will usually refer to the preceding day's trading only. Sometimes Monday papers have very little in the way of stock tables because the tables in the Sunday paper summarized the entire week's trading.

The closing price is always the price paid in the last transaction for that security during the trading period covered, no matter if it is a daily or weekly paper. Sometimes daily papers show the last prices as of a certain time (like 3:00 EST), if that particular edition goes to press before the exchange closes.

The two most common footnotes likely to appear here are:

u = means this price is a new high within the last 52 weeks.
d = means this price is a new low within the last 52 weeks.

The last column, called "change" or "net change," gives the amount that the closing price is changed from the closing price of the *previous* trading period. Like the price quotations, it is stated in points and fractions of points.

The examples show a standard format for stock quotations. Sometimes additional information will be given about dividends and earnings in weekly papers. Most frequently, however, less information will be shown. It is not uncommon, for example, for the 52-week high and low, the PE ratio, and the yield to be omitted.

Also, in the example above both dividends and earnings are

mentioned. They are easy to confuse. Don't forget that earnings are the profits of the company. Dividends, which are taken from the earnings, are the amounts the board of directors decides to return to the shareholders.

STOCKS TRADED OVER-THE-COUNTER

There are often as many as three different over-the-counter lists published in newspapers. Before discussing the actual quotations, some background is helpful.

There are two ways of disseminating information about the prices of OTC stocks and where they can be bought. The largest and most stable companies have their securities listed with the National Association of Securities Dealers Automated Quotation Service (NASDAQ). As with the exchanges, companies must meet certain requirements before their shares can be listed by NAS-DAQ.

The smaller companies, including those that don't trade frequently, those whose shares are not widely distributed, and new issues, will have their quotations listed in what are called the "pink sheets." This is a list (printed on pink paper) of stocks, their prices, and the brokers who deal in them. The pink sheets are distributed only to brokerages, and ordinary investors are not likely to encounter them. The only way to get a price quotation for one of these securities is to call a broker. Occasionally, a few stocks from the pink sheets make their way into a newspaper list under the heading of regional stocks. Even then, the list will be a small one.

It is the goal of small companies to graduate from the pink sheets to the NASDAQ system, although new issues of larger companies may be able to start out there. Almost 5,000 companies are listed. If it were an exchange, it would be the third largest stock exchange in the world (after the NYSE and the Tokyo Stock Exchange). As noted in Chapter Three, the NASDAQ system is a computer and telephone network. Brokers can punch up over-the-counter securities on their quote terminals and see the prices the various market makers (see below) are charging. They then call the broker whose price is acceptable and complete the transaction.

For over-the-counter stocks, market makers assume a role similar to that of the specialist on exchanges. These are brokers who "make a market" in particular stocks and "post" the prices on the NASDAQ computer system at which they will buy or sell the security in which they are making a market. Unlike the specialist system, however, there is no limit to the number of market makers. For popular stocks, there may be 30 or 40, and for relatively unknown stocks, only a few. The increased competition the market maker system fosters is generally regarded as beneficial in terms of price, liquidity (ease of buying and selling), and depth of the market (the ability of the market to absorb large buy or sell orders).

Incidentally, if you are thinking of buying an over-the-counter security, be sure to ask your broker how many market makers the stock has. If there are only two or three, you may be putting yourself in a precarious position. You are dependent on these market makers to establish the buying and selling prices, and there may be insufficient competition for a fair and healthy market.

Recently, NASDAQ has initiated a small-order service similar to the one for the New York Stock Exchange. Buy or sell orders for 500 shares or less can be sent to the NASDAQ main computer, and the market-maker offering the best price will be selected automatically.

In the newspapers, you will see one to three lists of NASDAQ securities. The main list is called the NASDAQ National Market, NASDAQ Stocks, or NASDAQ National Market Issues. Whatever it is called, the quotations are just like those for exchange-traded stocks, except that they leave out the yield percent and the PE ratio.

There are other lists, however, that are not quite the same. To explain them, we must first discuss bid and asked prices.

A *bid* price is the price at which a market maker (always a brokerage company) is willing to buy a stock. It is the price the broker is currently bidding to purchase specified amounts at that price. Often the quote will even state the specific number of shares the company is willing to buy at the quoted price.

An *ask* price is the price at which a brokerage company is willing to sell a stock. Until it is changed, this is the price at which a market maker is willing to sell a specified quantity of the stock.

When your broker punches up a particular stock on the NAS-DAQ system quote terminal, both the bid and the asked prices for the security are shown for each of the many market makers who are dealing in the issue. Your broker then scans the list for the best price—the highest bid price if you are selling, the lowest asking price if you are buying.

Market makers stand ready both to buy and to sell a specific security. Their bid prices are always slightly higher than their asking prices. Their profit comes from the spread between the bid and asked prices, by selling the stock at a slightly higher price than they paid for it. The bid or ask price is charged whether the customer is another brokerage or one of their own customers. Note that if your *own* broker is a market maker in the stock you want to buy or sell, *you will not pay a commission.* The profit your broker is making still comes only from the difference between the bid and the asked prices.

Some newspapers, in their over-the-counter quotations, list only bid and asked prices, as in the following example.

	①	②
	Bid	Asked
AMM Tel	$3^7/_{16}$	$3^5/_8$
Aecor	$^1/_8$	$^3/_{16}$
AfMd	$4^5/_8$	$5^1/_2$
AmJuel	$1^1/_2$	$1^5/_8$
AmLvng	$2^5/_8$	3

① **Bid price** is the price at which market makers (broker-dealers) are willing to purchase a stock. The quoted price is the bid price as of the close of trading.

② **Ask price** is the price at which broker-dealers are willing to sell a stock. The quoted price is the ask price as of the close of trading.

The size of the spread is usually a clue to the relative trading activity of the stock. If you have no other information from the quotation than the bid and asked prices, as in the above example, compare the spread, proportionally, to the spreads of the other issues listed. A relatively large spread can be a danger sign: The stock is probably not traded as frequently as other shares, and its price may be more sensitive to shifts in supply and demand.

Bid and asked prices are not unique to over-the-counter trading. They were mentioned here because they show up in the NASDAQ quotations that appear in the newspapers. Bid and asked prices are, in fact, a part of trading on all exchanges. A broker, in the two-way auction system described before, may say he has 800 shares of XYZ to sell at 20½. That is his asking price. Another broker may offer to buy the 800 shares at 20. That is his bid price. If the first broker says "I'll take 20¼," he has changed his ask price. If the second broker says "sold," he has upped his bid price to meet the ask price. We now have a transaction price, a price at which the trade actually takes place.

When exchange-traded stock is quoted in the paper, it is always the *transaction price* that you see. As we explained, bid and asked prices are also present, but they are not reported. On over-the-counter lists, except for the national market list, the bid and asked prices may both be shown (as in the example above), or only the bid prices may be given (as in the following example). Note that by showing the bid prices instead of the asked prices, the quotation tells you what the shares you may own are presently worth—that is, what someone will pay you for them. To buy shares, at the asked price, you will have to pay more than the bid price listed.

Stock & Div.	Sales 100s	Low	High	Last	Net Chg.
AA Computers	9	5½	5¾	5½	—
Adv Robots	31	4½	4¾	4⅝	+⅛
Aegos Serv	167	37⅝	37¾	37¾	+½
Ages Corp	691	14¾	15	14⅞	−⅜

① **High, low, and last** prices for any over-the-counter list other than the national market list are bid prices.

② **Net change** is the change, in points, of the last bid price of the trading period reported, compared to the last bid price of the previous trading period.

You will notice that as the stock prices get lower, the fractions shown in the quotations get smaller. Prices below $2 a share are shown in sixteenths, and below $1 a share, in thirty-seconds. The table here shows the dollar equivalent of all the fractions used in stock quotations:

DOLLAR/DECIMAL EQUIVALENCES OF FRACTIONS

FRACTIONS				DECIMALS
1/32				.03125
2/32	1/16			.0625
3/32				.09375
4/32	2/16	1/8		.125
5/32				.15625
6/32	3/16			.1875
7/32				.21875
8/32	4/16	2/8	1/4	.25
9/32				.28125
10/32	5/16			.3125
11/32				.34375
12/32	6/16	3/8		.375
13/32				.40625
14/32	7/16			.4375
15/32				.46875
16/32	8/16	4/8	1/2	.5
17/32				.53125
18/32	9/16			.5625
19/32				.59375
20/32	10/16	5/8		.625
21/32				.65625
22/32	11/16			.6875
23/32				.71875
24/32	12/16	6/8	3/4	.75
25/32				.78125
26/32	13/16			.8125
27/32				.84375
28/32	14/16	7/8		.875
29/32				.90625
30/32	15/16			.9375
31/32				.96875

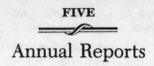

FIVE

Annual Reports

If you invest (or are thinking of investing) in stocks, bonds, or options, then annual reports are important reading. While annual reports, like most financial news, are usually taken for granted, reliable information about companies has not always been available to investors. It was only when complete disclosures were required by law (as in the Securities Exchange Act of 1934) that companies began to reveal their financial condition.

In earlier times, financial reporting was spotty at best, and frequently it was only members of the board (and those in whom they chose to confide) who had any real knowledge of the conditions of a corporation; it was considered no one else's business. Investors and their brokers frequently had to infer the health of a company from rumors, insider tips (which were not illegal then), and public actions such as acquisitions and foreclosures.

Today the Securities and Exchange Commission requires all corporations with more than 500 shareholders and more than $1 million in assets to publish an annual report within 90 days of the end of their fiscal year. The majority of companies are on a calendar fiscal year, making March the "season" for annual reports.

By the time you receive these reports, you may already have had a chance to see the earnings, sales, and a few other key figures in the capsule earnings reports that appear in newspapers. (These abbreviated reports are discussed in Chapter Six.) An annual report contains far more information than that, so you are missing most of its value if you look only at the earnings per share and net sales.

If you hold stock in a particular company, you automatically receive its annual report. If your shares are registered in your name (that usually means you have the share certificates in your possession), the company mails the report to your address. However, investors frequently leave their share certificates in the care of their brokers. It is convenient, and there is usually no charge for this service.

When you have your broker keep your shares, they are probably being held in "street name." That means the shares are registered in the name of your brokerage firm, not you. The company therefore sends the annual report, dividend, and proxy material to your broker, and it is that firm's job to forward this material to you. It may also hold your dividends in your cash account or forward them to you, according to your instructions. Brokers frequently hire a company that specializes in such services to distribute annual reports and to solicit your votes and proxy.

In the United States, brokers do not charge their customers to hold securities in "street name." In Europe and Asia, however, brokerages charge an annual safekeeping fee based on the value of the securities. There is no reason you shouldn't take advantage of this service, but you should know that if your broker goes bankrupt, your securities, even through they may be insured, will be frozen by the executor of the liquidating firm, and it will be an average of three months before you can get your hands on them. This means you cannot sell these securities during that time. Larger, well-capitalized security firms are usually safer, but you can avoid the potential problem altogether by having the securities registered in your own name and sent to you. The one disadvantage of holding your own securities is that when you sell these stocks you will have to return the certificates to the broker immediately, preferably by certified mail.

By the way, annual reports are not the only reports you will receive from companies whose stock you hold. Many companies distribute quarterly reports, and all explanations contained in this chapter apply to those reports as well.

When reading annual reports, it is important to remember that they are prepared by the companies about which they are reporting. It is only natural that those companies or their presidents will want to show their performance in the most positive light possible. After all, their audience is the shareholders (that is, the owners) as well as potential shareholders, investment analysts (who might recommend their stock for purchase), bankers (who might be asked for loans), and customers (whom they want to continue buying their products).

At any rate, one might think that tables and figures would leave little room for a "creative" presentation—for putting a good face on things. After all, the numbers have to add up and the balance sheet has to balance. But there are many ways a company can improve the appearance of its financial condition in its annual report. A blatant example would be a company that announces a 15-cent per share profit in its first quarter, when in fact it made that profit by selling a subsidiary on which a profit of 20 cents a share was realized. In this particular case, the announced 15-cent per share profit actually covered up a 5-cent per share loss.

How is one to ferret out this kind of information? There are two places it is likely to appear: in the president's message, and in the footnotes. Anything as blatant as the example above should appear in both, but certainly it would require a qualifying footnote and a listing of the sale revenue as an extraordinary item. In fact, all "creative" bookkeeping and unusual features of annual reports should be footnoted—and the footnotes are often where the real facts are revealed to those who bother to read them.

There is another financial report issued annually by companies called a "10K." It is a kind of no-frills annual report (typewritten) which is required to be filed with the Securities and Exchange Commission. Many analysts recommend that investors get a copy of it, too. It is available directly from companies by request. However, annual reports have become so comprehensive that for most purposes they are sufficient. In fact, often information is presented in tabular or graphic form in the annual report that you won't find in the 10K.

Finally, you might keep in mind that annual reports reveal the past, and what you want to know, obviously, is the future. You may want to know if now is a good time to buy stock in the company or if there is a chance that stock you already own will go up in price. You may only want to be reassured that your interest payments are secure. Whatever your reason, always look at the facts and figures in an annual report with this question in mind: "What does this mean for the future?"

Because of reporting requirements and bookkeeping standards, all pertinent information about a company's financial health is presented somewhere in the annual report. It is primarily a matter of knowing what to look for, and that is what this and the two subsequent chapters are about.

SECTIONS OF AN ANNUAL REPORT

The first step in making sense of an annual report is to understand its major sections and to know what kind of information to expect from each. Stock analysts who base their predictions on the past performance of a company take figures from different sections of the annual report and compare them with past years' figures, or they combine them to create new figures such as the book value, the acid test ratio, the payout ratio, and so on.

Many people mistakenly expect an annual report always to contain the market prices of the securities. Market prices of a company's stocks and bonds do not play a role in the finances of a company, since most of those transactions are on the secondary market. That is, the purchases and sales are between investors; the company is not involved, and it therefore receives no revenue from the transactions. If the company *itself* bought or sold its own securities, then an overall figure would be given for the total transactions. But that would still not constitute a history of the market performance. Sometimes, at the discretion of the com-

HIGH AND LOW BID PRICES
FOR XYZ COMMON STOCK

	1985	
	HIGH	LOW
First quarter	22½	18¾
Second quarter	20¼	17
Third quarter	19¾	16½
Fourth quarter	25⅞	17¾
	1984	
	HIGH	LOW
First quarter	17¼	15⅝
Second quarter	19¾	16⅛
Third quarter	18½	14¾
Fourth quarter	21¼	17⅜

EXAMPLE 1. MARKET PRICE OF SECURITIES AS SOMETIMES SHOWN IN ANNUAL REPORTS

pany, the annual report will contain a brief history of security prices—for example, the highs and lows for each quarter. Inclusion of such information, however, is not obligatory and is strictly up to the company preparing the report.

All major and minor sections of an annual report will be outlined briefly here. Several will be considered in detail either at the end of this chapter or in the two chapters that follow.

The President's Letter. This is partly a public relations tool. The president creates the image (e.g., one of prosperity, growth, honesty, or innovation) that he or she wishes people to have of the company. In doing so, valid reasons may be given for the company's performance (good or bad). Also, factors may be suggested which should be taken into consideration in the evaluation of that performance. Future goals or directions for the company may also be indicated.

The Balance Sheet. This is an accounting-type view of the company. The assets (what a company owns) are enumerated and weighed against the liabilities (what a company owes). One can get an idea of the size of the company from these figures. The difference between assets and liabilities is the owners' equity. It is a positive number if the assets outweigh the liabilities. When the liabilities are larger than the total assets, the company is said to have a negative net worth. That is, if the company were liquidated and all the money received used to pay the bills (assuming the money received was what the assets were valued at), there would still not be enough money to cover the liabilities of the company.

The Income Statement (also known as the *Statement of Operations* or the *Profit and Loss Statement*). This presents a picture of earnings and profitability for the last year. Where the balance sheet presents a picture of a company on one particular day, the income statement presents the cumulative report of the year's operations. Total income from sales is shown, as well as the costs of those sales. Here you will see if the company made or lost money from its operations. The per share earnings or loss figure will usually be found near the end of this statement.

Changes in Stockholders' Equity (also known as *Statement of Stockholders' Equity*). The stockholders' or owners' equity is the difference between assets and liabilities. Obviously, shareholders want to know how this amount has changed over the past few years. While it may have little to do with the market price of the stock, it is at least one concrete measure of the stock's worth. Figures for several years are presented so that you will see clearly whether the company is marching deeper into debt or if profits are being retained by the company.

Statement of Changes in Financial Position. The point of this statement is to show the increase or decrease in working capital. Many analysts consider it to be an important indicator of future performance, since the efficiency of daily operations depends on working capital, and problems in this area can mean increased debt.

Footnotes. Located near the end of the report, the footnotes explain figures throughout the other sections. It is typical that some of the most meaningful information in the annual report comes from this section. Any statement whose interpretation is not obvious from its wording or placement in the report will have a footnote.

Photographs. This is not a section of the annual report in the usual sense, but there is often a message here intended for the stockholder. Glossy photos, usually on the covers and immediately following the president's report, are selected to amplify the image of the corporation presented by the president. The message may be that the corporation is a great institution, that it has reliable and experienced leadership, that it is developing innovative products, or that it has hard-working employees. The important thing to remember is that whatever message is being relayed by photographs need have no basis in fact: Do not be misled by glossy photos.

Additional Matter. Frequently, you will see charts or graphs (sometimes extrapolated from figures in the report, sometimes not) that are of interest. For instance, a history of dividend payouts might be given. There may also be product descriptions or separate reports of the activities of various subsidiaries.

Accountant's Report. Usually labeled the "report of the independent certified accountant," this is one of the safety features of the report. The shorter the better—say, two or three paragraphs. Any warnings or qualifications here *must* be taken seriously.

THE PRESIDENT'S LETTER

Usually addressed "To our shareholders," the president's letter is always the first section of an annual report. While it is the president's job to present the company in the most favorable light, this doesn't mean that you need mistrust everything that is said.

If the company has had problems, some presidents take the direct approach: "We had a difficult year because . . ." This has the positive effect of creating trust on the part of the shareholders (the president is being forthright) and gives the impression that, while there are problems, management knows what caused them and is presumably doing everything possible to correct the situation.

Sometimes a useful perspective can be gained from the president's letter to assist in the interpretation of the tables to follow. This would be the case if you were to learn that the entire industry sector had been depressed or that a favorable foreign exchange rate augmented earnings. It is important, however, to remember to weigh such generalizations carefully.

If the president's promises seem too optimistic given the company's financial condition (or that of the economy), caution is in order. Be particularly careful of projections made in the annual reports of companies whose securities are known as "penny stocks" (extremely low-priced issues) and of small companies that have no track record.

Among the most important facts to be gleaned from this section is the future plans of the company. Such information often can be obtained nowhere else except at the annual meetings, which may not be convenient for you to attend. The company may be on the lookout for acquisitions. It may be changing its marketing strategy or its product lines. You need to consider statements of future plans carefully, in light of all that you know about the industry, other companies in the same business, and the economy in general. You might think that a nonexpert like yourself couldn't evaluate information of this kind, but you might be surprised at what you can discover with the knowledge of a few key ratios and by the application of a little common sense.

THE BALANCE SHEET

The balance sheet of an annual report gives a bird's-eye view of a corporation's financial condition. That's not an easy task, since a normal company's financial condition changes every day. When products are sold, the company deducts their cost from inventory and adds the sale price (presumably, higher than the production cost) to the accounts receivable. After the bill is paid, that amount becomes cash that can be used for any number of purposes, including starting the whole process over again. Both day-to-day activities as well as major shifts in the value of existing assets and liabilities contribute to a continually changing financial picture.

A balance sheet, therefore, takes one specific day (the last day of the fiscal year or the last day of one of the quarters) and presents a financial picture of the company as of the close of business on that date. If the corporation has subsidiaries, it will be called a "consolidated" balance sheet, meaning that figures for all subsidiaries are included in the total figure for the company.

The formula for the balance sheet is as follows:

$$assets \ = \ liabilities + owners' \ equity$$

In its simplest form, the assets are itemized and their value listed on the left, and the liabilities and owners' equity are itemized and shown on the right. The total on each side must be the same; that is, the two sides must "balance."

It is crucial that this formula be understood before proceeding further. Do not be misled into thinking that assets are "pluses" and liabilities are "minuses." We are dealing literally with the formula as is. If a company has $1,000,000 in assets and $600,000 in liabilities, then the owner's equity will be $400,000. It's as simple as that.

$$\$1,000,000 \;\; = \;\; \begin{array}{r} \$600,000 \\ +\$400,000 \\ \hline \$1,000,000 \end{array}$$

EXAMPLE 2

Another way of looking at it is that the owners (the stockholders) can lay claim only to those assets that are "clear"—not covered by debt (liabilities). That means the owners' equity is equal to the assets minus the liabilities (another way of stating the formula).

Here is an oversimplified balance sheet that follows our formula exactly:

BALANCE SHEET
XYZ CORPORATION
DECEMBER 31, 1986

ASSETS		LIABILITIES	
Cash	$ 100,000	Accounts payable	$ 50,000
Securities	200,000	Bank note	250,000
Inventory	150,000	Current liabilities	$ 300,000
Current assets	$ 450,000	Long-term loan	450,000
Factory	650,000	Total Liabilities	$ 750,000
Equipment	400,000		
Total assets	$1,500,000	STOCKHOLDER'S EQUITY	
		Common stock ($10 par)	$ 500,000
		Retained earnings	250,000
		Total stockholders' equity	$ 750,000
		Total liabilities and stockholders' equity	$1,500,000

EXAMPLE 3. ABBREVIATED BALANCE SHEET

The grand totals on both sides of the balance sheet are the same. Note that subtotals are shown, such as "current assets," below single lines, and the grand totals are shown above double lines. These are bookkeeping conventions that you will see in most balance sheets.

Balance sheets are usually too lengthy to be laid out in the fashion above (left and right), so the items are simply listed from top to bottom, as shown in our Example 4. A few more categories are shown than in the above example and they are explained below.

CONSOLIDATED BALANCE SHEET
ANY CORPORATION
DECEMBER 31, 1986

ASSETS

Cash	$ 210,000
Short-term investments	1,950,000
Accounts receivable	1,300,000
Prepaid expenses	325,000
Inventory	2,250,000
Other	75,000
Total current assets	$ 6,110,000
Property, plant, and equipment	$ 7,040,000
Intangibles	500,000
Total assets	$13,650,000

LIABILITIES

Accounts payable	$ 1,165,000
Accrued expenses	185,000
Accrued taxes	50,000
Total current liabilities	$ 1,400,000
Bonds (9% due in 2001)	1,500,000
Long-term loan	750,000
Total liabilities	$ 3,650,000

STOCKHOLDERS' EQUITY

Preferred stock (5%—par $50)	$ 500,000
Common stock (1$ par)	2,000,000
Additional paid-in capital	7,000,000
Retained earnings	500,000
Total stockholders' equity	10,000,000
Total liability and stockholders' equity	$13,650,000

EXAMPLE 4. SAMPLE BALANCE SHEET

We will now define some of the terms in Example 4.

ASSETS

Assets are everything a company owns. They include things you would expect, like factories and equipment, raw materials, and manufactured goods waiting to be sold (inventory). The company also owns its *accounts receivable*—that is, what is owed to it by other companies and individuals for goods or services already delivered. The accounts receivable are listed among the assets, even though they represent money the company has not yet received.

On a balance sheet, at least two kinds of assets are often

distinguished: current assets (which are usually listed first), and total assets.

Current Assets. These include cash and all assets which are likely, or at least able, to be converted into cash within the course of the year. The accounts receivable fall into this category, since payments for goods shipped to wholesalers or distributors are usually due within 30 to 90 days. The accounts receivable are reduced on the balance sheet by an allowance for bad debts, the portion of monies owed to the company it will never be able to collect.

Securities will be listed among the current assets (as they are in our example) if they consist of short-term instruments that are liquid or mature within the year. Any cash that the company does not need right away is usually put to work earning the highest return possible with the maximum safety. Government securities such as Treasury bills are popular for this purpose.

Prepaid expenses are items like insurance and rent, which are paid in advance. *Inventory* includes raw materials as well as manufactured goods in every stage of processing.

Values Ascribed to Assets. There are some important rules when it comes to listing the value of assets. For instance, securities held by the corporation have a value which is the price at which they were purchased, but they also have a market price as of the date of the balance sheet. They are listed on the balance sheet at whatever price is the lower. A footnote will usually give the other price.

The corporation has two choices when it comes to declaring the value of its inventory: FIFO and LIFO.

FIFO (first-in/first-out) means that when sales are made from inventory, the production cost attributed to the items sold is the production cost of the oldest items in the inventory. This usually means that the production cost will be the lowest possible, and therefore the difference between that amount and the amount received by the company is greater than it would have been the other way around. Thus the profit margin is slightly higher, but the value of the remaining inventory (cost of production) is also slightly higher.

LIFO (last-in/first-out) means that when sales are made from inventory, the value of the items sold is that of the most recent items produced and is therefore in line with the most current market conditions. This usually means slimmer profits, but lower production costs attributed to the remaining inventory.

For example, if a company has a four-month inventory of 1,000 tractors, those tractors produced four months ago may have cost less to produce than the tractors completed yesterday. If 100 tractors are sold today, it obviously makes a difference in calculating the profit on the sale whether the production cost of those tractors is figured at the price of the oldest tractors in the inventory or the youngest. By the same token, the value of the remaining inventory is also affected. In times of high inflation, FIFO is usually preferred.

If a company changes the method by which it evaluates its inventory, the value of its assets will change. A shift from FIFO to LIFO, for instance, could raise the value of the inventory, thereby raising the value of the assets and subsequently giving a boost to the owners' equity, even though nothing "real" has happened. When such a change is made from one year to the next, it must be noted somewhere in the annual report, even if in a footnote. Don't be misled by this kind of artificial raising or lowering of the inventories. That's not to say that a company would not have a legitimate reason for making such an accounting change, but you should be aware of the technique and understand its ramifications.

Quick Assets. Quick assets describes the total of all current assets minus the inventory. As stated before, current assets consist of items likely to be converted into cash within a year. In times of crisis inventories can be difficult to liquidate, so the concept of quick assets was developed to give a better picture of those assets which could easily be converted into cash under almost any circumstances. There are some cases where prepaid expenses may not be liquid, and those should not be included in quick assets.

Quick assets is the standard measure of a company's liquidity and shows how resilient a company would be in a crisis.

Fixed Assets. These are assets such as factories and machinery that help to generate income for the company. As such, they are not items produced for sale, but are fixtures essential to the ongoing operations of the corporation.

Depreciation. When factories and equipment age they wear out, become less efficient, and therefore decrease in value. Most fixed assets, therefore, are shown as declining in value over the years. Depreciation is the gradual (tax) writeoff of the purchase cost of the asset. However, it may or may not relate to the "disintegration" of the asset. In fact, a "fully depreciated" building may sell for more than its original cost. An amount attributable to depreciation is always deducted from the fixed assets before they are listed in the balance sheet.

Intangible Assets. These are assets which are regarded as having value by the company even through the assets themselves do not have a tangible existence. Goodwill (of suppliers, workers, customers) is in this category, as are patents and franchises. Amounts assigned in this category often appear to be arbitrary. If the value listed is as much as 20% to 30% of the total assets, this could be a signal that the company is short of "tangible" assets or long on liabilities.

LIABILITIES

Liabilities consist of everything owed by the corporation—all its bills. They are divided, like assets, into current liabilities and fixed liabilities.

Current Liabilities. These are obligations that should be paid by the corporation within the year. The interest due within the year on long-term obligations falls into this category.

Fixed Liabilities. These are obligations that mature or are expected to last longer than a year. Included are long-term loans and bonds issued by the company.

STOCKHOLDERS' EQUITY

As we said earlier, the stockholders' equity is the difference between assets and liabilities. But the story is a bit more complicated than that. You will usually find these four items listed under stock-holders' equity:

1. Par value of preferred stock
2. Par value of common stock
3. Paid-in capital
4. Retained earnings

Par Value of Preferred Stock. The dividend paid on a share of preferred stock is usually declared as a percent of the par value of the stock. Thus, a 5% preferred $50 par would pay a $2.50 annual dividend. Par is usually close to the amount at which the stock was originally issued, and obviously continues to have some effect on the market price of the stock. In this sense, preferred shares are similar to bonds. Par value is decided at issue and never changes.

Par Value of Common Stock. This has, over time, lost its original meaning. In fact, it has lost most of its meaning altogether. At one time par value was the initial price of the stock. Because of certain tax advantages, stocks for many years have been issued at a par value far lower than their expected initial market price. Many stocks are issued at no par value at all. Par value, then, is a relatively small amount of money listed in the stockholders' equity section of the balance sheet. At best it has some meaning when viewed in conjunction with the paid-in capital, since the two items together show the "nest eggs" acquired when the company went public and when (and if) there were subsequent stock offerings. Par value of common stock is decided at issue and never changes except through stock splits.

Paid-in Capital. This is the amount above the par value which the company received for the initial sale of stocks. This amount plus the par value of the common stock is the total capital raised by the sale of common stock. It is the nest egg the company gained by going public.

Retained Earnings. Sometimes called retained surplus, this is the profit kept by the company after paying out common stock dividends. When a company makes a profit, it can plow all the earnings back into the company (typical of growth stocks), give all of it to the stockholders in the form of dividends (typical of investment funds and mutual funds), or do some combination of the two. Most companies retain more of their earnings than they give to the stockholders in dividends. In this way a company can grow by increasing its capital base.

SOME IMPORTANT CALCULATIONS

There are a number of important calculations and ratios that can be determined on the basis of the balance sheet.

Book Value. This is an attempt to place a concrete value on common stock. It has nothing to do with the market value as stock usually sells in the marketplace at several times its book value.

To calculate the book value, take the stockholders' equity and subtract the value of the intangible assets (if any) and the par value of any preferred stock. Most intangible assets would be difficult to obtain cash for, and the preferred stock par value is an amount associated only with that issue, not with the common stock. Book value always applies to common stock, and by clearing out these other figures we now have a number into which you can divide the total number of common shares outstanding. This will give you the book value of each individual share.

This does not mean that you would get that amount if the company liquidated. As mentioned before, amounts attributed to the assets are attempts at fair and systematic evaluation, not at guessing what these assets would bring if sold in the marketplace. Thus book value can be said to be the theoretical value of the common shares *if* the assets of the corporation were liquidated at the amounts attributed to them on the balance sheet.

As with similar concepts, such as P/E ratios, this figure is helpful when comparing stocks in one company to stocks in other companies in the same industry. Should you spot a utility company, for instance, selling at a much lower ratio of price to book value than other utility companies, it might be an indication that you have discovered a good investment. The usual way of referring to book value is that a stock is selling for 5 times book value, 7.5 times book value, and so on. The lower the multiple, the greater the probable value of the stock.

Working Capital. Sometimes called net current assets, this is basically how much money the company has to operate with for the year. It is the difference between the current assets and the current liabilities. In other words, it is all the cash (including assets that will be turned into cash) available to the company after payment of all the bills.

Current Ratio. The current ratio is the number of times the current assets exceed the current liabilities. The usual formula is

$$\text{current ratio} = \frac{\text{current assets}}{\text{current liabilities}}$$

The current ratio is another way of viewing the working capital and is handy when comparing companies of different sizes. For example, the working capital of a small company could not meaningfully be compared to the working capital of an industry colossus, since even a small amount of working capital for the industry giant would be an enormous amount when compared to the needs of smaller companies.

As you might expect, different current ratios are normal for different industry sectors. In general, a ratio of 2 (that is, the current assets are twice the current liabilities) is considered acceptable. Some very conservative businesses, such as utilities, can get by on a current ratio of 1.

Acid test ratio. This is also known as the quick asset ratio or the liquidity ratio. It tells essentially the same story as the current ratio, but it is a more stringent test and preferred by some analysts. It indicates the relationship between the quick assets, not the current assets, and the current liabilities. (The quick assets are the current assets minus the inventory.) The formula is

$$\text{acid test ratio} = \frac{\text{quick assets}}{\text{current liabilities}}$$

HOW MUCH DEBT TO TOTAL CAPITALIZATION?

Many analysts feel that the relationship of long-term debt to total capitalization is the single most important fact to lift out of the balance sheet.

Total capitalization (Long-term Capitalization). This figure is obtained by subtracting the intangible assets and the current assets from the total assets. A rule of thumb is to be wary of any company whose long-term debt exceeds two-thirds of its total capitalization. Long-term debt, of course, is total liabilities minus current liabilities. You might check this figure for several years to see if the company is marching steadily into—or out of—debt. Younger and more aggressive companies usually have more debt in relation to their total capitalization than more established companies.

Again, compare the performance of several companies in an industry with respect to their debt to capitalization ratio. Low debt is not always good; it can mean that a company is not performing to its full potential.

Debt to Equity Ratio. Comparing long-term debt to stockholders' equity can be helpful in evaluating a company. If the long-term debt exceeds the stockholders' equity, it can be cause for concern. Such a situation is not uncommon for younger, more aggressive companies, but it can mean that the company will not be able to hold up if its fortunes take a turn for the worse. Such a company must continue to perform well to get its head above water eventually. More helpful here than the figures for any one year is the comparison of several years to determine a trend. If the shareholders' equity is growing faster than the long-term debt, obviously the company is headed in the right direction.

NET ASSET VALUE

Strictly speaking, the net asset value is simply the stockholders' equity. In the financial news it is always assumed to be presented on a per share basis. Therefore, the net asset value (NAV) is determined by dividing the stockholders' equity by the number of shares outstanding. One sign of a good value is when a stock can be bought for less than its NAV. Be careful when calculating this figure to divide with the number of shares that are actually outstanding, and not the total number authorized.

The NAV is particularly important to mutual funds, since that is at or near the price at which the fund will buy and sell its shares.

WHAT DOES IT ALL MEAN?

You will see references in the financial news to various of these balance sheet items and ratios, particularly in investment letters to which you may subscribe. In particular, analysts are sensitive to companies whose assets or ratios are not within industry norms or companies whose ratios have changed significantly from the previous year. Frequently analysts issue their buy and sell recommendations entirely on the basis of such observations. For example, a large amount of retained earnings and a high current ratio means that a company is cash rich. (Such a company is referred to as a "cash cow.") Often these are the companies that are selected as takeover targets by other companies which have uses for the cash.

SUMMARY OF CALCULATIONS TO BE MADE FROM THE BALANCE SHEET

Here is a quick review of the nine calculations mentioned in this chapter that can be made from the figures on the balance sheet.

Book value: Stockholder's equity minus the intangible assets and the par value of preferred stock.

Working capital (net current assets): Current assets minus the current liabilities.

Current ratio: Current assets divided by the current liabilities.

Quick assets: Current assets minus the value of the inventory.

Acid test ratio (liquidity ratio): Quick assets divided by the current liabilities.

Long-term debt: Total liabilities minus current liabilities.

Debt-to-equity ratio: Stockholders' equity divided by the long-term debt.

Net asset value: Per share value of the stockholders' equity. Divide the stockholders' equity by the number of shares outstanding.

Total capitalization (long-term capitalization): Total assets minus the intangible assets and the current assets.

THE INCOME STATEMENT

This section of the annual report has many names: Statement of Income, Statement of Operations, Earnings Report, Statement of Profit and Loss, to mention a few. No matter what it's called, however, the purpose of the income statement is to reveal how well the company performed last year by disclosing how much money was made (and from what sources) and how much was spent (and for what). The bottom line—profit or loss—is given for the entire year, both as a lump sum figure and as a per share amount.

Frequently the income statement appears first among the financial tables—that is, before the balance sheet. If you find yourself getting some of the tables mixed up, this one is easy to spot despite its many headings because the initial items listed will be "sales," "income," or "revenue." The term "sales" is used by the traditional manufacturing company that produces tangible goods. "Revenue" or "income" is used by companies that provide services, such as utilities, airlines, and banks.

Another characteristic of income statements is that data are given from at least the last least three years. This makes it possible to compare the most recent year's performance with that of previous years.

The balance sheet represents the condition of the corporation on one specific day. It freezes the corporation at the end of the fiscal year and takes it apart to see all its financial components. The income statement, on the other hand, is concerned with ongoing operations over a period of time—specifically, the flow of revenues and expenses during the previous year.

Keep in mind that the income statement does not reveal what is happening at the present time. The fortunes of the company at the moment you are reading the annual report could be quite different from those indicated by the income statement. The income statement does, however, present a relatively complete picture of what happened for the year just ended, and it is on this that you must base your expectations for the future.

EARNINGS PER SHARE

We will begin with a discussion of earnings per share (sometimes labeled "net earnings per common share") because that is what most people look at first. Investors seem to regard the earnings per share figure as a kind of "answer" to the income statement. But as with most answers, how one arrives at it can often tell more than the answer itself.

Earnings per share is derived by dividing the profit of a corporation by the total number of shares outstanding. The profit may be called "net profit," "net income," or "net earnings." It all means the same thing. This is the amount by which the total revenues exceed the total expenses for the year. The format of income statements may vary, but the earnings figure is usually found at or near the bottom of the table immediately following income taxes or a listing of extraordinary items.

If it turns out that the total expenses were greater than the total revenues, then the heading would be labeled "net loss." By bookkeeping convention, a minus figure is indicated by parentheses.

The net earnings figure represents the amount of money which is completely "clear," so that the board of directors has the option of plowing it back into the company, paying it out to the common stockholders as dividends, or a combination of both. Whatever amount is retained by the company should appear in the following year's balance sheet as an addition to the retained earnings figure.

As was said earlier, you are missing much of the meaning of the report if you only look at the net earnings figure. The meat of the statement is in the figures that precede earnings per share. Start at the top and see how the bottom line actually came about.

SALES, INCOME, OR REVENUE

The first items on the income statement will be labeled in one of the three ways shown above. "Net" sales is often used to indicate that deductions were made for price discounts (presumably to the wholesalers) or for returned goods.

Whatever the income is called, it is the major source of funds for the business. These funds are derived from the primary operations or functions of the company and its subsidiaries. Sometimes the entry will be labeled "revenues from continuing operations." Do not be misled by other acts of the company that may generate income, such as the selling of a subsidiary. Obviously, that subsidiary won't be around to boost the bottom line next year.

You may also see items listed as "income from discontinued operations." That is revenue from a business that has been sold or shut down. That income also won't be around next year. It is the ongoing income from the operations of the company that constitutes the backbone of the company.

COSTS AND EXPENSES

Following the list of all sources of income is the next major section: costs and expenses. If the costs and expenses are greater than the revenues generated, obviously a company will show a deficit unless there has been some other activity, such as a sale of property, to generate additional income. There are many ways the costs can be divided up. Here are some common ones:

Cost of goods sold (or cost of sales): This includes raw materials, salary of the labor force, cost of maintaining the factory, and other manufacturing-related expenses.

Selling and administrative expenses: These are all the expenses associated with the selling of the goods rather than with their manufacture. This would include salaries for the sales force, offices, commissions, and advertising expenses. Administrative expenses include salaries for other office staff and management.

Depreciation: This is a noncash item; the fixed assets against which the depreciation is charged may or may not already have been paid for. Depreciation is a bookkeeping method for spreading the loss of the value (figured as the purchase price) of a fixed asset over a period of years, whether that number of years relates to the actual useful life of the assets or the length of time the company actually takes to pay for the asset. One of the effects of depreciation is to reduce a company's taxes by means of a bookkeeping reduction of its taxable income.

Amortization: This is a kind of depreciation for intangibles. It represents the decline in the value of items like patents whose importance to the company may lessen over time.

INCOME (OR LOSS) FROM OPERATIONS

Sometimes this is listed as "operating income"; it may also be referred to as "gross profit." It is the result obtained when all operating expenses are deducted from the operating revenue (usually "net sales"). This is the profit from the operations of the company, but it is not the bottom line. To reach the bottom line, a number of other items have to be considered, such as income taxes, interest on bonds issued by the company, and revenues from extraordinary items or discontinued operations.

ADDITIONAL INCOME OR EXPENSE

A variety of items may be listed here that fall outside the usual activities of the specific corporation. The largest is often the sale of a subsidiary or of real properties when the gain from that sale is above the listed value of the properties. Income from stocks or bonds owned by the company may also be shown here, as well as loss or gain from foreign exchange and rental fees from unused properties.

Interest expenses are shown here too. This is the interest the company must pay on bonds it has issued or on bank loans.

EARNINGS BEFORE TAXES

Also called "income (or loss) before taxes," this figure is primarily helpful when comparing companies, one of which has a tax-loss carryforward (see below) that artificially boosts its earnings. If one of the companies has such an advantage, a simple comparison of earnings per share is misleading. Comparing earnings before taxes avoids the inequity.

TAXES

Companies are taxed on a sliding scale, much as individuals are. If the company does not make a profit, there are, of course, no taxes. A company with losses may have "tax-loss carryforwards." The IRS permits companies (individuals, too) to apply the losses of one year to successive years, thereby reducing taxable income during the whole period. Clearly this can help a company recover from a single bad year by permitting it to reduce or eliminate its taxes for a number of subsequent years.

Large tax-loss carryforwards are a valuable asset and can

make a company attractive as a takeover target, particularly by companies with substantial net income that would welcome such writeoffs.

NET INCOME OR NET PROFIT

All obligations of the company have now been met except those to the shareholders, both preferred and common.

PREFERRED STOCK DIVIDENDS

Preferred stock dividends (if any) are deducted at this point from the net income. This is why the stock is "preferred"; it has a claim on profits ahead of common stock.

NET EARNINGS AND EARNINGS PER SHARE

At last we are there. This is the clear profit. This is the money to be kept by the company or, in part or whole, paid back to the common stockholders in dividends. Sometimes it is even referred to as "earnings available for common stock."

You will see this figure in newspaper earnings reports. Per share earnings is the same thing, except that the net earnings is divided by the number of common shares outstanding.

Primary or Diluted. The earnings per share will usually be shown both primary and diluted if there have been investment instruments issued by the company (such as options, convertible bonds, warrants) that can be converted into common stock. Primary earnings per share is the earnings per share for the number of shares outstanding as of the beginning of the report period. Diluted earnings per share is the same thing except that it assumes all instruments with conversion capability were converted at the beginning of the report period. Diluted earnings must be shown if such a conversion could affect earnings per share by 10% or more.

Number of Shares. Most annual reports give the number of common shares outstanding somewhere in the report. Often it is the last item listed in the income statement, and both primary and diluted (postconversion) figures are shown.

Double Taxation. An important point mentioned earlier was that taxes are paid by corporations on earnings before dividends are distributed. This means that whatever money the investor receives in dividends has already been reduced by the tax bracket of the corporation paying the dividend. These dividends are then taxed again as individual income ("Income from Dividends" on the familiar 1040 form) for the shareholder. This is what is called double taxation.

SAMPLE INCOME STATEMENT

Example 5 shows a sample income statement. For simplicity, figures for only one year are shown. (In a real report you will see data for three years.) Review the descriptions of the parts of an income statement in this chapter and identify them in the example. Be sure you understand how those figures function in the

CONSOLIDATED STATEMENT OF INCOME
XYZ CORPORATION
FOR THE YEAR ENDED DECEMBER 31, 1985

Net sales		$10,000,000
Cost of goods sold	3,500,000	
Selling and administrative expenses	4,000,000	
Depreciation	500,000	
Amortization	100,000	
Total operating expenses		$ 8,100,000
Operating Income		$ 1,900,000
Other income		50,000
Income before income taxes and unusual items		$ 1,950,000
Equity in gain on sale of building		500,000
Income before income tax		$ 2,450,000
Federal, state, and local taxes	1,000,000	
Net income		$ 1,450,000
Earnings per common share		
Primary		$ .45
Fully diluted		$ .37
Average number of common shares		
Primary		3,222,222
Diluted		3,918,919

EXAMPLE 5. SAMPLE INCOME STATEMENT

balance sheet. Although not used in this example you should be aware that negative figures on some statements are shown in parentheses.

SOME HELPFUL CALCULATIONS

Just as there are a number of calculations you can perform on data from the balance sheet, so are there a number of calculations possible on the income statement that can help you make meaningful comparisons among companies.

Cash Flow. To calculate cash flow, take the net earnings and add noncash expenses and deduct noncash revenues. In its simplest form, this usually means only adding the annual depreciation to the net earnings. This makes sense in that the amount alloted for depreciation (or amortization) isn't actual cash spent, it's simply a bookkeeping entry. Dividends, both common and preferred, must be paid from cash flow.

Return on Equity. You will see frequent references to this ratio. It is derived by taking the net income and dividing it by the shareholders' equity (from the balance sheet). This tells you the return that management is realizing from the shareholders' equity. As long as it is above current interest rates, a company is doing fairly well.

P/E Ratio. The price earnings (P/E) ratio is quoted in many stock tables. It is the ratio of the per share price of the stock to the earnings per share. Many investors feel this ratio is the best indicator of the ongoing performance of a company.

To take a simple example, if a company had earnings per share of $2 and if the stock sold at $30 per share, the P/E ratio would be 15. Some industries, like utilities, have low P/E ratios (5 to 10), while growth companies may have P/Es of 30 or 40. Some foreign stocks (Japanese, for example) characteristically have high P/Es.

High P/Es are not always bad. If investors are willing to pay a high price for a stock in relation to its earnings, they must believe that the company has a bright future, that it will continue to strengthen and grow in the future. Buying a stock with a high

P/E is said to be buying a stock with a "high multiple." "Multiple" refers to the price of the stock being a "multiple" of the earnings per share.

A company with a deficit will, since it has no earnings, have no P/E ratio. In this case, since it has no earnings, the P/E space in the stock tables will be left blank. P/E ratios can also be relatively meaningless when a company is in or near a breakeven situation, with only a few cents of earnings per share.

Don't forget that common stock dividends come out of the earnings per share. A drop in earnings could mean that a dividend is in trouble.

SIX

Newspaper Earnings Reports

In the preceding chapter we took a look at annual reports, particularly the balance sheet and the income statement. If you own stock in U.S. companies, you will receive annual and quarterly reports from them. If you are interested in receiving annual reports and/or interim quarterly reports from a specific company and are not currently a shareholder, you can write to the corporate secretary at the company's headquarters. Although both annual and quarterly report requests are honored on an as-available basis, there are almost always enough. After all, it is in a company's best interest to encourage investor consideration of its securities. Actively traded stock at a healthy market price assures the company of strong market support for any new issues (stocks or bonds) it may contemplate bringing out.

Independent investors frequently request annual reports and current quarterly reports from several different companies within the same industry and compare the data carefully before selecting which securities they wish to purchase. Before annual or quarterly reports are mailed out, however, it is likely that newspapers will already have published at least some of the information in what we are calling "capsule earnings reports." The complete reports are made available to the newspaper wire services, but because of space limitations, only the three or four items that are considered to be the bottom line are usually reported. The annual and quarterly reports, when they finally reach you, are more valuable than these capsule reports, as they contain far more information. Nevertheless, the sales and earnings figures in the capsule earnings reports can be informative as a kind of preview of the reports to come, and an interested investor should know how to read them.

It might be helpful to say a word here about timing. If the price of a stock is to be affected by news of the company's earnings, then the rise or fall in price will take place immediately—the same day—as the earnings figures are made public by the company. Brokers and traders who keep a minute-to-minute watch for this kind of news will act on it right away. In fact, the action sometimes takes place before the final earnings report is available, particularly when the news is bad. An announcement that a company even *expects* a drop in earnings for the current quarter may be enough to cause a selloff of the stock before the actual figures are out. That selling pressure will drive the price of the stock down. However, in the securities markets there are no certainties. There are also cases where the price of the stock has gone up when the official "bad news" finally came out, either because it wasn't quite as bad as it might have been, or because of relief that the worst might be over.

For the investor who takes the time to read and analyze an annual report, the challenge is to extract enough information about the company's past to predict future trends. Those items in an annual report that interest the analysts are those with implications for the future profitability of the company and, by extension, the price of its shares. If a company's record shows promise, and this promise has not yet been recognized by a significant number of other investors, buying its stock may get you in on the ground floor of a substantial capital appreciation. However, it may be months or even years before the promise is realized or other investors agree with you and start buying the stock too. Nevertheless, a prudent investor is willing to acquire the stock early and is prepared to wait.

Although the usual reason for analyzing an annual report is to decide whether or not to buy a particular stock, annual reports should also be examined from the point of view of protecting one's current holdings. For instance, if you already own stock in a company and its earnings are declining, or it is marching steadily into debt, you may want to consider selling unless you can find a reasonable justification for the negative development or an indication that it is a short-lived phenomenon. After all, why hang on to equities which at best are going to go nowhere, when you could put the money into safe debt instruments like U.S. Treasury bonds that will give you an assured income?

For the short term, analysis of the annual report is not much help. Generally, the positive or negative implications drawn from an annual report will take some time to develop. Therefore, if you determine your investing strategy through analysis of the company's performance, you must be prepared to hold your securities for long-term gains. Incidentally, investors who invest in this manner are called "fundamentalist," because these are the "fundamentals" they are following.

CAPSULE EARNINGS REPORT

Let us take a look at some sample reports. The first one provides only the most basic information. Even so, note that data are given for two years so that current performance can be easily compared to last year's.

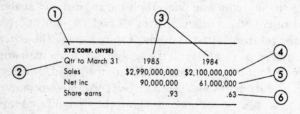

XYZ CORP. (NYSE)		
Qtr to March 31	1985	1984
Sales	$2,990,000,000	$2,100,000,000
Net inc	90,000,000	61,000,000
Share earns	.93	.63

① **Name of the company,** usually shortened, and the primary market on which its common shares are traded.

② **Time period of the report.** It is cumulative for the year, so a third quarter report would be, in effect, a nine-month report.

③ **Years of the figures given.** Those for the previous year are always from the same period of time (number of months) as the present report.

④ **Sales figures in dollars.** The amount is always net, allowances having been made for discounts and returns.

⑤ **Net income in dollars.** This is the profit after payment of all obligations except dividends for the common stock.

⑥ **Share earnings.** This is the net income divided by the number of shares outstanding. It shows how much of the earnings is represented by each share of stock issued.

The reports are usually cumulative within the year. Thus, if you are looking at a second quarter report, it may first have figures only for that quarter, but it will be immediately followed by a six-month report that includes the data for the first two quarters together. The same is true of the third quarter, which will have data for nine months and, of course, the fourth quarter, which is the annual report.

The figures for the previous year will always be for the same relative time period in order to make meaningful comparisons. It would be confusing to have a six-month report for the current year with only yearly figures from the previous year with which to compare them, especially for a company whose business is seasonal, with annual cycles from quarter to quarter.

These reports are listed entirely from the annual or quarterly earnings or income statement, so items from the balance sheet like assets will not be found. If you want to know the current price of the security you must, of course, go to the stock tables and look for the quotation on the exchange indicated. If you are interested in preferred stock, you should know that sometimes preferred issues do not trade on the same exchange as the common shares. If the security trades over-the-counter, there are sometimes as many as three different OTC lists in the newspapers which you must check.

In our example, sales are up $890 million compared to the same quarter last year ($2,990,000,000 minus $2,100,000,000). That's an increase of 42%. The next thing to ask is whether the profit (net income) has also kept pace with this high rate of increase. Increased manufacturing costs, for instance, could keep the profit from rising by the same percent.

As the next line shows, the profit rose from $61,000,000 to $90,000,000. That's an increase of 47.5%, and this company has done extremely well. There is only one thing further to ask: Has an increase in the number of shares outstanding decreased the percentage increase on a per share basis? For instance, if the number of shares that a corporation has outstanding doubles in a year, then the per share earnings will be only half of what they would have been if the number of shares had not been increased. This phenomenon is known as dilution.

If a company has issued more stock, or if convertible securities have been converted to common shares in any significant numbers, this fact is supposed to be included in the capsule report. (You will see a later report where this is the case.) There are variations, however, in the comprehensiveness with which newspapers report these earnings, so you may want to verify the number of shares outstanding for yourself.

In our example we can see that the current per share earnings figure is $.93. That's a 47.5% increase over the previous year's figure of $.63, and is the same percent increase as in the total earnings figure. There has been little or no dilution.

By dividing the per share earnings figure into the net income, we can get a rough idea of the actual number of shares outstanding. In our example, using the latest figure, $.93 goes into $90,000,000 about 96,774,000 times, which is the approximate number of shares issued and outstanding.

THE P/E RATIO

If the earnings statement you are looking at is for a stock traded over-the-counter, the newspaper capsule report won't have the P/E ratio. Since the per share earnings figure will be included in the earnings statement, you can calculate the P/E ratio by dividing the current price of the security by the per share earnings. You must be careful, however, *always* to use an *annual* figure for the earnings per share.

In our example, the $.93 per share earnings is for the first quarter only. We would have two choices for determining the annual ratio. First, we could assume that the company is going to perform exactly the same for the next three quarters. That would make an annual per share earnings of $3.72 ($.93 × 4). If the stock were selling at $50 per share, the P/E ratio would be 13.4 ($50.00/$3.72). On the other hand, we could take the earnings from the prior three quarters and add them to the current quarter and calculate on that basis.

If you have quarterly reports from the previous year, it is better to use those earnings to determine the P/E ratio. But let's assume that the only information we have is what we see in this report. Last year, the first quarter earnings per share were $.63. For the second, third, and fourth quarters (which are the ones needed), we could take a straight-line average between $.63 and

$.93 to interpolate what the earnings for those quarters might have been: $.70, $.78, $.86. The total of those three quarters and the most recent one ($.93) is $3.27, a somewhat more modest figure than $3.72. Again, if the stock were selling at $50 per share the P/E would be 15.3, almost two points higher than the P/E calculated earlier. As mentioned earlier, the lower the P/E, the higher the presumed value you are getting for your money if you purchase the stock.

Both of these calculations made use of a lot of guesswork. If our report had been a second-quarter six-month report, we would have had to estimate only earnings for the previous two quarters, and from a third-quarter report we would have had to guess only at the last quarter previous to the currently reported year. However, if you were seriously considering investing in that security, you would want to get the actual earnings figures for the previous three quarters from the last annual report.

NET PROFIT MARGIN

One other calculation might be helpful before leaving our first example, and that is the net profit margin. It is the net income (after tax) as a percent of net sales. It is derived by dividing the net income by the net sales. If we divide the 1985 net income of $90,000,000 by the sales of $2,990,000,000, we arrive at a profit margin of 3%. That's not a very large profit margin. While we have seen that the profits are increasing, there is still room for improvement unless this company is in an industry, like electric utilities, that traditionally has a low profit margin. The following

XYZ CORP (NYSE)		
13 wk Apr 1:	1985	1984
Sales	$11,265,000	$15,170,000
Net loss	65,000	b177,000
Shr earns:		
Net loss	—	b.05
39 weeks:		
Sales	$37,554,000	$47,646,000
Net income	a354,000	1,824,000
Shr earns:		
* Net income	.11	.55

a—includes a pretax nonrecurring charge of $258,000 for settlement of litigation.
b—income.

earnings report contains data for the current quarter and a cumulative report for the last three quarters.

This report is more complex than the previous example. Look at the second item in the first quarter, labeled "Net loss." In the first quarter of 1985 (the third quarter of this company's fiscal year), the company's expenses outweighed its income, producing a net loss—the amount the company went into the hole. The comparable figure for 1984 is footnoted with a "b." Below the report we see the "b" means that the figure is income, so that money was not lost the previous year. Footnotes of this kind are used frequently in abbreviated earnings reports to save space, since otherwise there would have to be another line labeled "net income" for the $177,000 figure.

The third item is the "Shr earns," the earnings per share. In 1985 there was a loss and, for reasons that are not hard to understand, "loss per share" amounts are sometimes not given. You can figure it out for yourself if you know the number of shares outstanding (see below).

In the 1984 column, the "b" footnote reminds us again that the $.05 figure is an earnings per share amount. If you wanted to know the number of shares outstanding in 1984, you would divide the $.05 into the net income of $177,000 to get 3,540,000 shares outstanding. You have no way from this report of determining whether the number of shares remained constant in 1985, since no comparable "per share loss" is given.

Note the remaining footnote, "a" in the 1985 39 weeks net income column. That tells us the company lost a lawsuit sometime within the nine months of the report (although not in the most recent three months), and the amount lost was deducted so that only the net figure is shown here.

The most important information to be obtained from this report is that both sales and profits are down, both in the third quarter (when compared with the third quarter of last year), and cumulatively for the three quarters (when compared to the three quarters of earnings and sales of the previous year).

Since the 1985 nine months' report shows a profit of $354,000, you can assume that money must have been made during the first two quarters of that fiscal year, and that is the profit which absorbed the loss of the third quarter.

Sometimes newspapers present the earnings data in tables such as the one in Example 2. Although they save space, such a format does not allow for footnotes, extraordinary items, and other qualifications that would not fit into the format.

SALES AND EARNINGS REPORTED

		SALES ($ MILS)		NET PER SHARE	
COMPANY	PERIOD	1985	1984	1985	1984
Ascot labs	12 months	2,340.00	2,040.00	2.01	1.73
Acid Chem Co	6 months	34.80	31.20	0.82	0.68
Air Clean	3 months	373.60	366.40	NA	NA
Aldona Inc	12 months	1,190.00	1,050.00	0.95	0.40
Albert Cutlery	3 months	81.00	69.90	0.38	0.29

EXAMPLE 2. EARNINGS REPORT IN TABLE FORM

Note that sales are stated in millions, so that 2,340.00 is actually $2,340,000,000. Also, in the third company you see an "NA" in the earnings columns. Standing for "not applicable," it indicates that there were no earnings—that is, the company operated at a loss for those three months.

Example 3 shows the use of parentheses as a bookkeeping convention to indicate negative numbers. The use of parentheses is inconsistent from paper to paper, so be careful to determine how the convention is being used in the reports you are examining. Here the net loss and per share loss for the previous year are shown in parentheses.

WIDGET TECHNOLOGIES, INC.

40 WKS. JAN. 3

	1985	1984
Revenue	$36,613,000	$41,012,000
Net income (loss)	186,000	(3,253,000)
Per share (loss)	.37	(1.05)

EXAMPLE 3. EARNINGS STATEMENT
THAT USES PARENTHESES FOR
NEGATIVE NUMBERS

Parentheses are not always used for negative numbers. Sometimes, when a line is labeled "loss," the figure will appear as a positive number.

Some papers present only the net earnings and the per share earnings for the last two years (see Example 4). This, of course, neglects sales figures and any extraordinary items, but it still gives the investor a "bottom line" to work with until the annual report itself arrives.

CORPORATE EARNINGS

YEAR ENDED DEC. 31

	1985	1984
Alderon Inc	$81,000,000	$44,692,000
per share	$7.04	$3.44
Auto Turn Intl	20,231,411	18,552,397
per share	2.44	2.26
Blight & Smith	8,757,000	5,836,000
per share	2.49	1.68
Chico Corp	94,475,000	86,041,000
per share	3.40	3.07

EXAMPLE 4. EARNINGS REPORT
SHOWING ONLY NET AND PER
SHARE EARNINGS

SEVEN

Takeovers, Mergers, and Tender Offers

Among those conditions known as special situations, few have the power to move the price of stocks like mergers and takeovers. So dramatic are the opportunities for substantial profits that some traders direct the major part of their investment strategies toward the acquisition of the stocks of companies that may be (or already are) merger or takeover targets.

MERGERS AND TAKEOVERS

Mergers can take many forms and may be subject to many different requirements, depending on state regulations and on the restrictions and stipulations of the target company's certificate of incorporation. Generally, however, a merger requires ratification by a stated percent of the shareholders. That percent may range from 51 to 75, again depending on state regulations and the certificate of incorporation. If the merger proposition does not meet with the objections of the board of directors, and if it is ratified by the shareholders in a merger vote, there is obviously cooperation of the target company, and the entire process is referred to as a merger.

Takeovers, which happen over the objection of the board, will eventually require a merger vote too. If the takeover company has acquired enough stock and/or convinced enough stockholders to accept the takeovers, perhaps even selling their shares in the process, then the merger will eventually be ratified by vote —but the entire process is referred to as a takeover.

The usual procedure for a takeover is through the purchase of stock in the target company. Stock might be acquired through open market purchases, private transactions, or a tender offer

National Chemical Merges with Suburban Propane Gas

NEW YORK—National Chemical Corp. said it completed acquisition of Suburban Propane for $200 million. Suburban Propane is to be operated under "current management" said a spokesman for . . .

American Distributors Attempts City Outlets, Inc., Takeover

SEATTLE—American Distributors launched a hostile takeover of City Outlets, the Kansas City clothing chain, by offering $25 per share for all City Outlets common shares. . . .

Calico Co. Plans Tender Offer To Raise Stake in Trinity Manufacturing

NEW YORK—Calico Co., the principal party in a group that holds nearly 15% of Trinity Manufacturing, said it plans a $16-a-share tender offer to enlarge the group's interest to about 26%. . . .

A merger is the acquisition of one company by another, usually through the purchase of enough shares in the targeted company to constitute controlling interest. Rarely is it two companies mutually acquiring one another.

A takeover, like a merger, is the acquisition of a company through purchase of a controlling amount of its stock. The word "takeover" usually indicates that the attempt is over the objection of the board of directors of the target company. Takeovers are thus forced mergers. Stock in the target company may be acquired by open market purchases, private transactions, or a tender offer.

A tender offer is an open offer made by a company or an individual to purchase the stock of another company at a stated price and by a stated time. In order to attract the number of shares desired (which will be specified, or the offer will say "any and all"), the tendering company must offer to purchase the shares at a price that is attractive to stockholders—that is, at a price above their current market value. A tender offer is often, but not always, the first step in a merger or takeover attempt. In this example the stated purpose is to enlarge Calico's stake in Trinity Manufacturing, but it is probably a prelude to a takeover.

(discussed later). When enough stock is acquired by the takeover company, the objections of the board of directors won't make any difference.

The use of the word "merger" is somewhat misleading. It is rare that two companies mutually absorb one another, one becoming indistinguishable from the other. A merger is a takeover—albeit a friendly one; it is one company acquiring another. When a takeover attempt runs into serious objections from the board of directors of the target company (not just a request for a higher per share price), it is referred to as a "hostile" takeover.

In the first example here, use of the word "merger" indicates that the two companies are in accord. Specifics are not reported, but presumably the purchase price of $51 per share was found to be acceptable to the board of Suburban Propane, Inc. In the second sentence of that story we see that Suburban Propane will continue to operate under the same management, so it is also safe to assume that retention of the management of the target company was among the agreed-upon items.

The terms of a merger may be many and complex, and all are subject to negotiation, both before and during a merger attempt. The most important points are usually those concerning the offering price for the securities and the future of the target company and its management. If there is resistance to the initial offering price by the stockholders or board members, the price may be raised (called "sweetened"). In this way, many initially hostile takeovers have been transformed into friendly mergers.

Opposition by the target company's board of directors will have some effect, even if they do not directly control a large number of shares. One of the most common ways to resist a takeover is to insist (true or not) that the shares of the company are worth more than the price being offered. This is sometimes effective in reducing the number of stockholders who will offer their shares to the takeover company for purchase.

The amount of stock needed to gain control of a company is not always a majority of the common stock outstanding. Sometimes the stock is so widely dispersed that a voting block of far less than 50% can effectively control the company. Also, a company's articles of incorporation may define controlling interest as more or less than 51%.

In recent years, companies have shown great ingenuity in escaping the clutches of unwanted suitors. You will see a number of colorful terms in the financial news referring to some of these practices.

Poison Pill. This antitakeover measure adopted by the board of the target company is designed to make the company "hard to swallow." The company might, for instance, threaten to issue preferred shares at an unusually high dividend rate or conversion privilege. Once issued, such shares might be awkward to recall, if not illegal, depending on the conditions of issuance.

One interesting attempt involved issuing warrants to current shareholders that, in the event of a hostile takeover, could be redeemed for shares of the acquiring company at half price. Truly a poison pill, it is being challenged in court.

White Knight. Sometimes a company cannot resist a takeover attempt alone and resorts to offering itself to another company that it considers more suitable. The more suitable company is known as a white knight.

Shark Repellent. The company's defenses might be enhanced by any number of measures so long as they are not prohibited by law or by the certificate of incorporation. The directors could even try amending the certificate of incorporation to permit additional defense measures if they feel they have sufficient votes to do so. They might try an amendment requiring a supermajority (say, 75%) ratification of any merger proposal. They might issue options on the remaining shares held by the company. They might even try buying up company shares in the open market.

Golden Parachute. Board members worrying about losing their jobs as a result of a takeover can contrive for themselves something known as a "golden parachute." It usually consists of lucrative bailout measures such as fat severance pay or stock allowances in case of a takeover. The fears of such executives are well founded. One study has shown that when a company is taken over, 52% of all executives leave the company within three years —even when the merger is friendly.

WHY DO COMPANIES ACQUIRE OTHER COMPANIES?

Among the most logical acquisitions are those where the assets or operations of the target company complement those of the takeover company. A large manufacturer, for example, might acquire a company with a source of needed raw materials, or it might acquire a packaging company or a chain of retail outlets. Almost any extension of present operations can make sense so long as antitrust laws are not violated.

Economic conditions (like high interest rates) or regulatory changes (like *de*regulation) can make one industry sector more attractive than others. For instance, when restrictions on banking operations were relaxed, discount brokerages became popular takeover targets for banks and insurance companies.

Diversity is another reason for acquisition. This becomes particularly appealing to a company that sees limited growth potential within its present sphere of activity. But whatever the reason, it is frequently easier, and even cheaper in the long run, to buy a complete company that brings with it needed operations, assets, and employees, rather than attempting to build or to develop those assets from scratch.

WHAT IS A TENDER OFFER?

The offer to purchase stock in another company comes in the form of a tender offer. This is a public offer to purchase a specified amount of a company's stock at a stated price, and by a stated time. Such offers may constitute either the first or the second step in a takeover, or they may simply be acquisitions for investment purposes. In the Calico example, the stated purpose of the tender offer is for investment purposes. However, 26% is a large holding in any company. It is probable that Calico, the acquiring company, will at least seek representation on the Trinity Manufacturing board. And, of course, should it decide to do so, Calico is already more than halfway toward owning 51% of the stock.

A tender offer, by virtue of its public nature (by law, it must be advertised) and because it must attract a sufficient number of offers to sell stock, will usually have to offer a price for the stock well above its current market value. The usual marketplace reaction to a tender offer is an initial leap in the price of the stock, but not all the way to the level of the offering. (There is still the possibility that the takeover will fail.) For instance, if an offer is at $10 above the current price, there may be an initial leap of anywhere from one to five points. In fact, the degree to which the market price approaches that of the tender offer can be an indication of professional traders' opinions as to the takeover's chances of success. Should the takeover fail, the stock's price will probably fall back to where it was before the attempt was made.

Unfortunately, by the time you, the investor, hear about a takeover bid, the price of the stock will have already risen substantially, and it will probably be too late to buy shares and participate in the biggest portion of the increase. This is because professional traders see notices (on their quote terminals or news services) about mergers and takeovers as soon as they are made public. Newspaper articles *you* read will already be a day old, and television reports you watch will probably be at the end of the day, after the markets have closed.

More important than their edge on the financial news, brokers and professional traders also have sophisticated research facilities that enable them to spot probable takeover targets. And, on a lesser technological level, professional traders are also finely attuned to a more arcane form of communication: rumor. Rumors about takeovers can spring up on as little as a report of messenger service between two corporate headquarters, or on something more substantial, like the landing of XYZ's corporate jet on another company's airstrip.

No discussion of mergers would be complete without mention of "insiders." These are people who act on inside information to reap huge profits in the stock or options market. While there is a fine line between a rumor and inside information, an insider "knows" the information he or she has is reliable and uses it for personal profit. An insider is defined as an officer, director, or principal stockholder of a corporation or a member of such a person's immediate family. The definition has been extended to include even persons with access to inside information. For instance, the typist who types up a merger document would be in violation of the law if he or she were to act on any of this information or pass it on to others.

If you think that all this puts the ordinary investor at a tremendous disadvantage when it comes to playing takeover strategies, you are right. In fact, speculation in this area is best left to professionals. However, you can put a general knowledge of the mechanisms of mergers and takeovers to good use in two ways. First, you may be in the lucky position of already owning the stock of a company that becomes a takeover or merger target, in which case you will know what course of action to take. Second, you may initially select your investments with an eye toward their eventual attractiveness as takeovers. If, in the latter case, you restrict your purchases to companies that are also sound investments (not easy when you are playing takeover strategies), then should your companies *not* become takeover targets you will still have good investments to show for your trouble.

Another type of tender offer mentioned earlier is a company's offer to repurchase its *own* shares. Such a course of action would be undertaken for a variety of reasons; it would increase the value of the shares outstanding (fewer shares outstanding means higher earnings per share), or it could lessen the chance of a hostile takeover attempt, since the shares purchased would no longer be available to a takeover company. Another reason could be that a company simply feels that its shares are undervalued relative to the market.

HOW DOES A TENDER OFFER WORK?

You may first hear about a tender offer through an article or through a "tombstone" advertisement in a newspaper. If you own stock in the target company of a merger, you need not respond to an advertisement; by law, you must receive a copy of the offer in the mail. In fact, it is better to wait until the last minute to tender your shares because other (better) offers may be made before the original one expires.

The tender offer you receive in the mail will contain a form to fill out and return to the company making the offer (or its agent). It will state the offering price, the deadline by which time the form (not the share certificates) must be postmarked, and any other special circumstances of the offer.

It is usually to your advantage to tender the stock. Its price may never reach the tender offer level on the exchanges. Also, after the merger, the price of stock in the target company often sinks to the pretakeover level, assuming it trades independently of the parent company at all.

Sometimes a tender offer is for a combination of cash and stock, or even an outright exchange of securities (called a swap). If over 50% of the tender payment is in stock, taxes will not have to be paid on the stock portion until it is sold. All cash received from a tender offer, whether constituting a complete or partial payment, is subject to capital gains tax, long-term or short-term, depending on how long the security has been held.

WHAT IF ANOTHER OFFER IS MADE?

Sometimes tender offers will spark other offers, which of course will be at a higher offering price than the existing offer. Should you have already tendered your stock to the first company you may, on the second set of forms you receive (from the second company), withdraw your previous offer and tender your stock to the second company *if the deadline on the first offer has not expired.* Should you have purchased stock in the company after news of the first tender offer, then a rival bid such as this will probably guarantee you a profit, if the second offer is successful.

WHAT CAN GO WRONG?

A number of things can prevent you from receiving the full tender value for all your stock. First of all, tender offer contracts invariably have "outs": conditions under which the tendering company will not accept any of the stock offered. The most common of these is that an insufficient amount of stock has been tendered. Although there might still be an advantage to acquiring the targeted stock, the tendering company may want to back out if the takeover cannot be achieved.

It is also possible that the target company can successfully defend itself. One of the worst ways to do this, from a stockholder's point of view, is for the target company to buy back the shares (at a higher price) that were previously acquired by the takeover company. In this situation, known as "greenmail," the takeover company usually extracts a huge profit, and the takeover target has less cash—or worse, newly acquired debt—to show for its troubles.

Another common development that might keep you from receiving the amount you expect from a tender offer is that the offer could be oversubscribed.

WHAT IS OVERSUBSCRIBED?

When more stocks are tendered than the amount stated on the tender offer, the offer is oversubscribed. The acquiring company may still purchase all the stock tendered, but it has the option of purchasing only the amount required; however, it may take it from *all* the shareholders on a pro rata basis (an equal proportion from each shareholder). Thus, if you tendered 1,000 shares and the company needed only three-fourths of the total shares offered, it could purchase only 750 shares, and you would keep the remainder. Sometimes there is another offer made to purchase any remaining shares at a lower price. It could be advantageous to sell the remainder, even at a lower price, since the sale would not incur a broker's fee. All tender offer transactions are without brokerage fees.

PROXY FIGHTS

The proxy fight is another tactic for gaining control of a company, and it has the advantage of being much cheaper than buying shares outright. If an investor or group of investors can reach enough of the major shareholders of a company and convince them to vote against management or to give their proxy over to the dissident group, then such a shareholder or group of shareholders can gain control of a company. Obviously, this method is not as airtight as actually owning the shares, and the cooperative shareholders might be persuaded to change their minds again. Nevertheless, some stunning victories have been won by dissident shareholders through proxy fights. A proxy fight doesn't usually mean big profits for the shareholders, but if successful it may mean new management for a company, and that could have long-range benefits for the market price of the company's stock.

HOW TO SPOT A TAKEOVER TARGET

A number of conditions make a company attractive as a takeover candidate. Of course, just because a company meets one or more of these conditions does not mean that another company will automatically come along with the money to acquire it.

Being cash rich, as explained in Chapter Five, often makes a company attractive. That fact, along with general economic conditions, should be kept in mind when looking for takeover targets.

Sometimes an acquiring company may quietly amass a significant position in another company by gradually buying up its shares in the open market. This kind of activity is an important sign to watch for. Gradual purchases might go unnoticed if it weren't for an important requirement of the Securities and Exchange Commission which states that any company acquiring 5 percent of the outstanding stock of another company must report this information to the SEC in a 13D filing. Such filings are watched by the investment community and the press. Almost invariably, on a 13D filing the acquiring company will claim that the acquisition is for investment purposes. But usually there is some kind of escape clause that leaves the way open for another course of action such as an eventual tender offer. And such changes of intention can occur on very short notice.

EIGHT

The Dow Jones Industrial Average and the NYSE Composite Index

Many indexes and averages track the performance of groups of securities. All the national and regional stock exchanges have their own indexes, the major reporting companies like Standard & Poor's and Value Line have long-established indexes, and there are indexes for specific industry sectors such as utilities, health care, transportation, and financial services.

Of all the indexes and averages pertaining to the stock market, none receive as much attention in the financial news as the Dow Jones industrial average. But before we look at this popular market indicator in detail, there are a number of preliminary issues to consider.

First of all, what's the difference between an "average" and an "index"? At one time there were sufficient divergences to distinguish between them, but with time they have become obscured. The only difference today is that the term "index" seems to enjoy greater popularity with the inventors of new market indicators.

Among all market indicators, whether averages or indexes, an important distinguishing feature is their focus—that is, whether they are broad indicators or narrow. Take, for example, two well-known indicators, both of which are made up of stocks listed on the New York Stock Exchange. One is the Dow Jones industrial average, and the other is the New York Stock Exchange Composite Index. The former consists of 30 major blue-chip stocks and is thus one of the narrowest of all major indicators. The latter is made up of all common stocks listed on the New York Stock Exchange. It is a broad-based indicator; in fact, it couldn't get any broader, since it takes into its calculations every stock of the group which it covers.

THE DOW JONES INDUSTRIAL AVERAGE

The Dow Jones Company, publisher of the *Wall Street Journal,* computes and publishes four stock price averages. They are the Dow-Jones industrial average, made up of 30 industrial stocks; the utility average, made up of 15 utility stocks; the transportation average of 20 transportation stocks, and a composite average of all 65 stocks.

In the beginning, the averages simply gave the arithmetic mean of the prices of all the stocks in each index. This became more and more complicated as stocks split, companies acquired other companies, and some companies were dropped and others were substituted. Increasingly complicated formulas were devised to compensate for these changes and avoid distorting the data.

Stock indexes and averages are tools to be used in technical analysis. Investors who put faith in them assume that the future course of security prices can be determined by their past performance. When this thinking is applied to individual stocks, the analyst believes that factors outside the company are usually more important in determining the future price of the securities than factors *within* the company. In other words, to anticipate what the price of a stock will be, you do not look at the company (its annual report, its products) as a fundamentalist would do. Instead, you look only at a chart of its past prices. Hard-line technicians sometimes pride themselves in not knowing what the companies in which they invest do. They work solely from graphs of the price performance of the stock. This is an extreme position, however, and most analysts tend to take *all* aspects of a company and its securities into consideration.

The technical approach to investing has most frequently been helpful for determining the timing of a transaction, either a purchase or a sale. For long-term investment, it has proved less than satisfactory.

Technicians feel that major moves in stock averages or indexes tend to perpetuate themselves until they are countered by decisive changes in the market. This is because investors tend to buy when the market is going up and to sell when the market is going down. Such activity has the added benefit of enhancing the very trends it recognizes, since additional sales in a down market drive prices even lower and additional purchases in an up market will move prices even higher.

A close reading of stock indexes, and particularly the Dow Jones industrial average, is thought by many to have implications far beyond the prices of stocks. Charles Dow himself felt that the Dow averages would indicate the beginning and the end of both bull and bear markets. He did not use the averages to predict the performance of any one specific stock, but to recognize major turns in the market and to forecast changes in business cycles or general business conditions.

People all over the world think of the Dow Jones industrial average as representing the New York Stock Exchange, if not the entire United States securities market. It doesn't literally, of course; it is a narrowly based blue-chip indicator. Strictly speaking, it isn't even "industrial" any more, as it contains securities from the high-tech and financial sectors.

One of the reasons for the popularity of the Dow Jones industrial average is that, dating from 1884, it is the longest-running stock average in the world. At its inception, the industrial average contained only 12 stocks. The securities marketplace has changed a great deal since then. The transportation average, for instance, is thought to be far less important than when the health of big railroads reflected the state of the economy. Also, many feel that the service sector is not adequately represented. Nevertheless, the Dow Jones industrial average has yet to be superseded by any other indexes, despite their comprehensiveness or claims to accuracy in market forecasting.

Technical analysts interpret the Dow Jones industrial average as an indicator of future stock market trends by comparing the peaks to which the average rises, and the points to which it drops. For instance, a bull market is in progress when each intermediate peak is higher than the previous one and each intermediate low is also higher than the previous low. Likewise, a bear market is in progress when each intermediate peak is lower than the previous high and each intermediate low is also successively lower.

Such clear trends are expected to continue until there is a clear change in market conditions.

Of more importance to investors than confirmation of major (and obvious) trends is the indication of new trends. For instance, the possibility of a bull market is signaled when the intermediate bottoms start to rise, even though the peaks are holding relatively steady. If, for three weeks in a row, the DJIA bottoms were 1,000, 1,006, and 1,015, investors would begin to look for a market turnaround even though the peaks might still be descending. When the peaks begin rising too, then a bull market is confirmed.

The possibility of a coming bear market is indicated when intermediate peaks start to fall, even though the bottoms are still rising. When the bottoms begin to fall too, the bear market is confirmed.

Here are the companies that, at the time of this writing, make up the various Dow Jones averages.

STOCKS THAT MAKE UP THE DOW JONES STOCK AVERAGES

INDUSTRIALS (DJIA)

Allied-Signal	General Electric	Owens-Illinois
Aluminum Co.	General Motors	Philip Morris
American Can	Goodyear	Proc. & Gamble
American Express	Inco	Sears Roebuck
AT&T	IBM	Texaco
Bethlehem Steel	Intl. Harvester	Union Carbide
Chevron Corp.	Intl. Paper	United Tech.
Du Pont	McDonald's Corp.	US Steel
Eastman Kodak	Merck	Westinghouse
Exxon	Minn. M&M	Woolworth

TRANSPORTATION

AMR Corp.	Delta Air Lines	Santa Fe So. Pac.
Amer. Pres. Cos.	Eastern Air Lines	Transway Intl.
Burlington North	Federal Express	TWA
CSX Corp.	NWA Inc.	UAL Inc.
Canadian Pacific	Norfolk Southern	Union Pac.
Carolina Freight	Overnite Trans.	USAir Group
Consolidated Freight	Pan Am. Corp.	

UTILITIES

Am. Elec Power	Consol. Nat. Gas.	Panhandle E. Cp.
Cleveland E. Ill.	Detroit Edison	Peoples Energy
Colum-Gas Sys.	Houston Indust.	Phila. Elec.
Comonwealth Edison	Niag. Mohawk P.	Pub. Serv. E&G
Consolidated Edison	Pac. Gas & El.	Sou. Cal. Edison

THE NYSE COMPOSITE STOCK INDEX

The NYSE Composite Stock Index was established in 1966 and provides a comprehensive measure of market trends on the New York Stock Exchange. It is made up of four subindexes: the industrial, the transportation, the utility, and the finance indexes.

In order to represent changes in the aggregate market value of NYSE common stocks with as little distortion as possible, it is necessary to eliminate the effects of changes in capitalization (such as stock splits) as well as the addition of new issues and the removal of others.

The method used in this index is to multiply the per share price of the stock by the number of shares outstanding. Thus the total amount of equity dollars represented by all shares of each issue can be determined. This total market value (the sum of the total market value of all common stock issues listed on the NYSE) is then expressed as relative to the market value *when the index was initiated in 1966*. An arbitrary value of 50 is taken as the base value for that year, and the movement of stock prices is measured from there. The arithmetic procedure, greatly oversimplified, is to take the current total market value of all the listed securities, divide that sum by the market value of all listed securities in 1966, and to multiply the results by 50.

Changes in the NYSE Composite Index are reported every half hour on ticker tape, and they are available to traders even more frequently. Besides a general pulse of the market, the index provides the base for options written on the index and for futures contracts (see Chapter Fourteen).

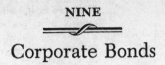

NINE

Corporate Bonds

Bonds are loans. They are often called "debt instruments" to distinguish them from stocks, which are "equity instruments." If you buy a bond you are, in effect, lending money to the issuer of the bond. In return, the issuer agrees to pay you interest at a stated percent and to return the principal to you at maturity.

In principle, bonds are simple. But there are so many varieties and special circumstances under which they are issued that the average investor usually knows far less about bonds and the bond marketplace than he or she knows about stocks or stock markets.

When a company wishes to raise capital, it has three major recourses (other than to increase profits or liquidate assets). It can sell more stock (discussed in Chapter Three); it can borrow from a bank; or it can issue bonds (which is tantamount to borrowing from the public—or whoever buys the bonds).

With bonds, a company enters into a contract to borrow a fixed overall amount which is secured by specific assets or by the credit and reputation of the company. A fixed annual amount of interest is pledged, which is stated as a percent of the par value of the bond. The par value is the amount at which the bond is denominated. (It is also known as the "face value," or "principal amount," and is printed on the front of the certificate.) The interest is distributed to bondholders in two semiannual installments. When the bonds mature (on a specified date), the par value of the bond is returned to each bondholder, and the "loan" is canceled.

If a corporate bond is not backed by a specific asset (such as buildings or equipment), it is called a "debenture." The credit-worthiness and good name of a company stands behind these

Flormar Co. Offers 8.5% Bonds

HARTFORD—Flormar Company, the second largest textile manufacturer in the U.S., is offering $200 million in 8.5% bonds due in 2010. A spokesman for the . . .

Bonds are loans, usually in $1,000 denominations. They pay a stated interest rate (the coupon rate), and at maturity the principal amount (par value) is returned to the bondholder. The coupon rate is the rate of interest paid on the face amount of the bond. The coupon rate never varies except with a floating-rate bond.

The maturity date is when the principal is returned to the bondholder.

Beachman 8% Bonds Priced to Yield 10%

MIAMI—Because of an unexpectedly low credit rating, underwriters for the Beachman 8% bond, due to mature in 2006, have priced the bonds to yield an . . .

"Priced to yield" means that the price has been adjusted over or under the par value (usually $1,000) so that the amount the bond pays will, in fact, constitute a different percent yield on the amount invested than the coupon rate.

Ratings —credit ratings are given each company and each bond by Moody's or by Standard & Poor's. Such a rating is intended to reflect the creditworthiness of the issuer and its ability to meet the obligations of the bond.

Bond Prices Rise on Drop in Interest Rates

NEW YORK—Bond prices, responding positively to the recent lowering of interest rates, rose to their highest levels in the last . . .

Bond prices are directly linked to interest rates. When interest rates fall bond prices rise, and vice versa. This keeps interest yields for older bonds in line with current interest rate levels.

issues. With major companies, that is usually enough to provide reasonable security for the prudent investor.

Bonds are given a rating by at least two different credit rating services. These ratings, to be discussed later, enable an investor to make a decision with regard to the safety of specific issues and the creditworthiness of the issuing company at the time of the rating. Obviously, these ratings can be no guarantee of the future performance of the company.

If a company whose bonds you own goes bankrupt, you should know that the claims of debtors always come before the claims of owners. In the securities business, this means that if a company liquidates, the principal amount of all bonds is remitted to the bondholders before any distribution is made to stockholders. But while the claims of bondholders to the assets of a company are senior to those of stockholders, there are often several issues of bonds, and some issues are senior to others. Only a broker or a bond guide, such as *Standard & Poor's Bond Guide,* can help you sort out the priority of bond issues. If you stick to reasonably safe and creditworthy companies, the problem of the seniority of bond issues should never arise.

In the first example, the Flormar Company is offering bonds to investors with an 8.5% coupon rate. That is the percentage rate the bond issuers will pay on the face value of the bond. The term "coupon rate" dates from the time when most bonds were in bearer form. The owner (bearer) of the certificate was assumed to be the owner of the bond, and there was no registration with the issuing company. Interest payments could be obtained only by clipping the "coupons" attached to the bond certificates and sending them in to the company. Whoever sent in the coupons got the interest payments. This permitted a certain amount of anonymity for bondholders and invited tax evasion for bonds that were not tax exempt.

Although many municipal bonds are being traded that are still in bearer form, all new bonds issued after 1983, whether corporate or municipal, must be in registered form. A registered form bond requires that the owner of the bond be registered with the bond issuer or his agent. This means that interest payments can be mailed automatically, and there is no further need to clip coupons. Nevertheless, the term "coupon rate" has persisted.

As you can see later in the article, Flormar is seeking to raise $200 million. The complete offering will therefore consist of 200,000 bonds denominated at $1,000 each. Bonds can be denominated in other amounts, such as $5,000 or $10,000, but if there is no indication, the denomination is assumed to be $1,000.

The 8.5% specifically means that the bond will pay $85 a year in two $42.50 semiannual installments. If you pay the par value for the bond, your yield will be exactly the coupon rate, 8.5%.

However, by the time bonds are actually issued the initial asking price may change, thus causing the yield to be different from the coupon rate. The company never pays anything but the coupon rate on the par value. The market price of the bond, however, can be either above or below $1,000.

This is what has happened in the case of the second example. There we can see that the bonds issued by the Beachman Corporation have an 8% coupon rate, meaning that they will pay exactly (and only) $80 a year in two $40 installments for each $1,000 bond. The company, however, received a substantially lower credit rating than the underwriters expected, so they have priced the bonds at $800 rather than $1,000 (this does not alter the fact that the par value or face amount is $1,000). Even though the amount was not mentioned in the article, we can tell that the asking price was $800 because the $80 annual interest would constitute 10% only of $800.

WHAT DETERMINES THE PRICE OF A "SEASONED" BOND?

All prices listed in newspaper bond tables are for "seasoned" bonds. After a bond's initial purchase it becomes seasoned, and its price is no longer set by underwriters. Like all other financial instruments, its price is determined by the forces of supply and demand in the marketplace. However, those forces are different for bonds than they are for stocks.

We have mentioned three different values associated with bonds: the face or par value (usually $1,000); the initial price asked for a bond (which is set by the underwriters and to an extent determined by market pressures and the credit rating of the company); and the market price for the seasoned bond (which fluctuates daily with supply and demand).

An important factor that affects the initial price and the market price of a bond is the credit rating of the company. The lower the rating the higher interest rate the company is expected to pay, since presumably the risk to the investor is higher. This is a classic example of the interdependence of yield and risk. The higher the risk, the higher the yield should be.

There are two companies that both institutional investors and individuals rely on to keep track of the financial health of companies that issue bonds. This is important not only when a company first issues bonds, but in the subsequent years when the company is expected to meet regular interest payments, and at maturity when the principal amount is to be returned to bondholders.

The two companies that rate all major corporations in the United States are Moody's Investment Service and Standard & Poor's. Their rating levels are roughly equivalent, although the symbols they use are somewhat different. Both rate the same corporations, and their ratings are usually the same or close. The following table gives a condensation of the category definitions and the equivalent ratings.

Within each category gradations are possible with pluses and minuses for Standard & Poor's, and with arabic numerals for Moody's. A significant lowering of its credit rating, due to poor earnings, increased debt, or any number of factors, can cost a company millions in additional interest *should it decide to issue new debt instruments.*

There is an important distinction made among the categories. Some are considered "investment grade," and others are not. For a bond to be investment grade, it must be considered safe for both individual and institutional investors. Standard & Poor's lowest investment grade rating is any among the BBB levels; Moody's lowest investment grade rating is any among the Baa level.

Once an issue of bonds is sold, the lowering of the credit rating may not immediately affect the company, since it continues to pay the same interest on its bonds that it contracted to pay. The immediate loser is the bondholder who, if he or she sells the bond, will receive a lower price than was paid (when the company had a better credit rating). Of course, if the bonds are kept they will continue to yield the same amount of interest. But the principal is presumably at slightly higher risk, a fact for which the bondholder is not compensated. The company does not begin to feel the effects of the lower credit rating until it tries to borrow again. Then, as explained earlier, the rates it has to pay will be higher.

Ratings are not shown in the newspaper listings, but you can clearly see their results in the yield columns. Those bonds with the highest yields, comparatively, are those that have the lowest ratings.

BOND RATINGS

STANDARD & POOR'S	MOODY'S	APPROXIMATE MEANINGS
AAA	Aaa	Highest quality
AA+	Aa1	High quality
AA	Aa2	
AA−	Aa3	
A+	A1	Upper medium quality
A	A2	
A−	A3	
BBB+	Baa1	Medium quality
BBB	Baa2	
BBB−	Baa3	
BB+	Ba1	Speculative
BB	Ba2	
BB−	Ba3	
B+	B1	Very speculative
B	B2	
B−	B3	
CCC	Caa	Poor quality, may be in default
CC	Ca	Highly speculative
C	C	Poorest quality
D	D	In default

Supply and demand do not play as important a role in bond prices as in stock prices. Whenever there is an increase in demand for a bond it can affect the price, but that demand is usually the result of other determinants more germane to bond prices themselves, such as a rise or fall in general interest rates. Movement of a company's stock prices does not in itself generally affect bonds. A drastic fall in stock prices, of course, could be the result of financial trouble within the company, and that could lead to a lower credit rating, which in turn could lead to lower market prices for that company's bonds.

Interest rates are an important factor in the movement of the price of bonds. If you received $100 interest on a new bond, the coupon rate would be 10%. However, if interest rates fell and comparable bonds began yielding 7%, then you could sell your bond for a capital gain if you wished to do so. This is because your bond would be yielding more than the current rate of 7%. The price of your bond would be adjusted upward in the marketplace until the $100 approximated the 7% standard yield for bonds of similar quality. In short, you might sell the bond for as high as $1,428, depending on its credit rating. A bond that sells at a price above its face value is said to sell "at a premium."

One of the fundamental relationships in finance is that between interest rates and bond prices. When interest rates go up the prices of seasoned bonds go down, and when interest rates go down the prices of seasoned bonds go up. This adjusts the yield of a seasoned bond to current interest rate levels, enabling the yield of seasoned bonds to approximate the yields of new bonds of the same type and credit rating.

A less obvious factor in bond prices is the maturity date. If a bond is selling at a "deep discount" (investment jargon for selling far below the face value) but will mature in one year, the investor would receive the stated yearly interest rate but would also reap a huge capital gain, since the face value, not the market value, is returned by the company at maturity.

Let's take an example. If a $1,000 bond with a 7% coupon rate were selling at $800 and were maturing in one year, the bondholder would receive $70 interest for the year and $1,000 at maturity. The maturity payment would be $200 higher than the market price paid, making a total profit of $270, a 27% gain in one year.

Clearly such a bond would not sell for $800 (unless it had a terrible credit rating). The prices of all deeply discounted bonds that are near maturity are bid up so that the combination of the interest payment and capital gains equals a profit appropriate for the credit rating of the bond. What this means is that the closer the bond is to maturity, the closer its price begins to come to the face value.

YIELD

We have already discussed the current yield. It is the percentage that the annual interest payment constitutes of the amount paid for the bond. As you can see from the discussion of maturity dates, the current yield doesn't tell the whole story. Another yield is calculated, called the "yield to maturity," that takes into account the following factors:

1. The price paid for the bond relative to its face value (the capital gain or loss you stand to make at maturity)

2. The time left until maturity (when you will receive the capital gain or loss)

3. The coupon rate which you will receive in the meantime

Yield to maturity is particularly helpful when comparing the yields of bonds with different coupon rates, different maturity dates, and selling at different discounts or premiums. It is not usually found in newspaper quotations, but you will see it in bond guides, and of course your broker will know.

Calculation of the yield to maturity is complex because it attempts to arrive at a single percentage figure to represent both current yield and a capital gain or loss to be realized at some time in the future. For instance, if you were trying to decide on whether to buy an 8⅞% bond due in 7 years for $970 or a 6% bond due in 18 years for $595, it would be helpful to know that the yield to maturity on the first is 9.45% and for the second is 11.28%.

TYPES OF BONDS

SECURED BONDS

Unsecured bonds are called "debentures." Secured bonds come in various types, depending on the nature of the security. The major varieties are as follows:

1. *Mortgage bonds,* backed by the mortgage of real property.

2. *Equipment trust certificates,* backed by the mortgage of equipment such as trains or airplanes.

3. *Collateral trust bonds,* backed by securities of another company, on deposit.

CONVERTIBLE BONDS

Convertible bonds may be exchanged (converted) into a set number of common shares of the issuing company. Their prices tend to follow interest rates, like other bonds, except for times when the market price of the stocks into which they can be converted exceeds the par value of the bond.

For example, if a $1,000 bond could be exchanged for 20 shares of a company, the bond would be worth $1,000 only so long as the interest rates remained the same and the per share price of the stock was below $50. As soon as the stock price rose above $50, the price of the bond would track that of its value when converted into shares. If the shares reached $60, the bond would be worth at least $1,200 (perhaps more, considering that the interest rate was probably greater than the dividend payments of the stock).

Bond tables in the newspapers do not usually indicate the type of bond, but convertible bonds are an exception since there are circumstances, as described, under which the price of these bonds does not perform "normally." Thus, in the newspaper bond tables you will see a "cv" in the yield column to designate convertible bond issues.

OTHER TYPES

Two other types of bonds that you may see in the news are zero-coupon bonds and floating rate bonds.

Zero-Coupon Bonds. These are bonds that sell at a deep discount and pay no interest (thus the term "zero coupon") until maturity, at which time they pay the face amount to the bondholder. This produces sizable capital gains at maturity. Investors are taxed yearly, however, on the interest (which they haven't received), amortized over the time until maturity. These bonds are popular in IRAs, where the tax does not apply.

There are two interesting varieties of zero-coupon bonds created by major brokerage houses: CATS and TIGRS. CATS stands for Certificates of Accrual on Treasury Securities, and TIGRS stands for Treasury Investment Growth Receipts. Both are zero-coupon bonds backed by long-term U.S. Treasury bonds held by the issuer. They represent ownership of future interest and principal on a pool of Treasury bonds where the interest payments have been separated (stripped) from the main bonds. In essence, the investor has bought Treasury bonds at a deep discount with the interest payments separated from them. What one pays for is the capital to be received in the future upon maturity of the bond.

One of the appeals of zero-coupon bonds is that the investor doesn't have the burden of reinvesting the dividends of these bonds at possibly lower interest rates. Yield to maturity has been calculated on hypothetical reinvestment at the same (coupon) rate of interest. Thus zero-coupon bonds are debt instruments that, through compounding, lock in a specific interest rate for the total invested amount, including the interest.

Floating Rate Bonds. These are bonds whose interest rates rise or fall if general interest rates, or certain key indicators, rise or fall substantially. They are particularly appropriate for investors who fear interest rates are going up and who don't want to lock in a current low rate.

BOND QUOTATIONS

Here is a typical bond quotation as you would see it in a local newspaper. The 12-month high and low shows the total range of prices paid for the bond within the last twelve months. Most people do not think of bonds as instruments on which they can realize capital gains, and it is true that prices of bonds are not as volatile as those of stocks. Nevertheless, there is still a considerable price range, as reflected in the 12-month high and low, and thus there is a possibility for selling bonds for more (or less) than you paid for them. This kind of a situation develops automatically, of course, in periods where rising or falling interest rates cause the price of bonds to move significantly.

Prices of bonds are quoted in percent of par. It is assumed that all bonds are in $1,000 denominations, so that a price of 87½, as a percent of $1,000, means $875. This is different from the point system used in stock quotation.

Note that the name of the company, in the second column, is followed by the coupon rate and the year of maturity. The first example would therefore be the XYZ bond, 10% maturing in 1997.

The next column is the current yield. That is the percent that the fixed annual interest constitutes of the purchase price. Thus, while the first bond has a 10% coupon rate, since the current price (under "last") is 83¾, $83.75 makes a current yield of 11.9%.

Note that if you own a bond, its current yield does not vary. You will have locked in whatever yield was current at the time of purchase, and that will be your yield for the bond as long as you own it.

The "Sls in $1,000" column is the number of bonds sold, all denominated in $1,000. The high, low, and last columns are the same as for stock quotations except that, as stated before, the quotations are in percent of par.

Likewise, the net change is in percent of par: +1 means +$10 for a $1,000 bond.

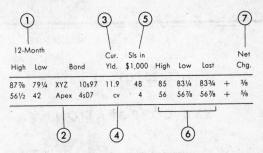

| 12-Month | | | Cur. | Sls in | | | | Net |
High	Low	Bond	Yld.	$1,000	High	Low	Last	Chg.
87⅞	79¼	XYZ	10s97 11.9	48	85	83¼	83¾	+ ⅜
56½	42	Apex	4s07 cv	4	56	56⅞	56⅞	+ ⅝

① **Highest and lowest prices** paid for bond in last 12 months. Prices quoted in percent of par—e.g., 87⅞ for a $1,000 bond = $878.75.

② **Name of bond,** usually abbreviated, followed by the coupon rate, in percent, and the year of maturity. The "s," when used, is a convention from the way dealers refer to bonds—e.g., XYZ 10's of 97 (that is, 1997).

③ **Current yield** is the percent yield the annual interest amount constitutes of the current price—i.e., the price in the "last" column. This is the annual percent yield you will receive if you buy the bond at the closing price.

④ This indicates a **convertible bond** which may be "converted" into a specified number of common shares of the same company.

⑤ **The number** of bonds sold during trading period covered.

⑥ **Prices paid** for the bond during the trading period covered. Prices are quoted in percent of par value.

⑦ **Change,** quoted in percent of par, of the closing ("last") price of this trading session and the previous trading session.

BASIS POINTS

Discussions of bond yields will frequently mention "basis points." This is the standard unit of measurement for the specification not only of bond yields, but of movement in interest rates and foreign exchange rates.

One basis point is equal to one-hundredth of a percent (.01%). Thus the difference between bonds yielding 8.3% and 8.4% annually is *10* basis points, while the difference between 8.32% and 8.36% is 4 basis points. Note that this is a different way of expressing yield from the fractions used in the percent-of-par quotations typical of newspaper bond quotations.

Since the difference of 1 basis point for a corporate bond (assuming $1,000 denominations) is only 10 cents in the course of

---

① **$125,000,000**

XYC CORPORATION ②

9½% Debentures due February 15, 2006   ③

Silverman Bank International   ④

Transylvania International Limited

Bank of Anytown

First National Bank of Paradise

---

① Total amount of borrowing. If the bonds are all in denominations of $1,000 then the total issue will consist of 125,000 bonds.

② Name of company issuing the bonds.

③ Coupon rate and maturity date.

④ Underwriters conducting initial marketing of the bonds.

a year, you may wonder why the standard unit of measurement is so small. Bond merchants, however, routinely deal in millions of dollars. And from the point of view of the issuer, a difference of a few basis points in the coupon rate of bonds can mean a difference of hundreds of thousands of dollars annually.

NEW ISSUES

New issues of bonds are advertised in "tombstone" ads something like stocks. At left is an example of such an ad.

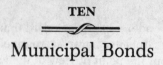

TEN

Municipal Bonds

Municipal bonds are debt instruments issued by states, political subdivisions of states, and certain other authorities or agencies within states. "Political subdivisions" include cities, towns, and counties. "Authorities or agencies" include almost any municipal entity that might undertake a public work like a hospital, toll road, nuclear power plant, sewer system, even a college dormitory. Usually, such works produce a facility that will generate income at some point in the future, income which will in turn be used to help the municipality meet interest payments as well as the return of the principal at maturity.

Before going further, we should make it clear that municipal bonds are not issues of the U.S. government; they must be issued at the state level. In fact, it is the affiliation with the state that gives them their tax exemption. In 1895 the U.S. Supreme Court ruled that interest from state municipal instruments was exempt from federal taxes. That was, of course, a great victory for states rights. The benefit to the states (and their municipalities and agencies) is that they can borrow money at a lower interest rate than they would otherwise have to pay. The reason for this is that the tax-free dollars they pay in interest are worth more to investors than dollars which will be taxed. For those in the 50% tax bracket, every dollar received is the equivalent of two dollars on which taxes have to be paid. But no matter what your tax bracket (assuming it is above zero), a tax-free dollar is worth to you the amount you would have to earn in order to keep that dollar after taxes. For instance, if you are in the 23% tax bracket, you still have to earn about $1.30 in order to keep $1.

Municipal Bond Prices Surge

NEW YORK—Major brokerage houses have reported sharp increases in demand for tax-exempt bonds. . . .

Municipal bonds are bonds issued by states, political subdivisions of states, and specific authorities within states.

Tax-exempt bonds are municipal bonds. The term refers to the fact that interest from these instruments is exempt from federal income tax. They are also usually exempt from state and local taxes, if any, depending on state and local regulations.

Hospital Bonds to Yield 6% Tax Free

SAN DIEGO—Bonds issued by the Municipal Hospital Authority were priced at par today to yield 6% tax free, their coupon rate. Underwriters have expressed . . .

Tax-free interest refers to interest from municipal bonds. It's value to the investor varies depending on the investor's tax bracket. For instance, if you were in the 30% tax bracket a 6% tax-free yield would be the equivalent of an 8.5% taxable yield.

One of the easiest ways to get an idea of what a tax-exempt bond is worth to you is to figure out what an equivalent yield would be in a corporate bond. That is, what percentage interest would you have to earn from a corporate bond in order to have, after taxes, the same amount of money you would get from a municipal bond?

Here's a formula that figures it out for you. It is an important formula, because you will always have to make this calculation for yourself. You will not see it in the financial news, because the corporate equivalent yield depends entirely on your own personal tax bracket.

$$\frac{\text{tax-exempt yield of bond}}{100 - \text{your tax bracket}} = \text{equivalent taxable yield}$$

Let us say that you see a tombstone in the paper advertising a new tax-exempt bond selling at par with a coupon rate of 7.5% and you are in the 30% tax bracket:

$$\frac{7.5}{100 - 30} = 10.72\%$$

Thus a municipal bond that yielded 7.5% would be equivalent to a corporate bond that yielded 10.72%. That is, in both cases you would be able to keep the same amount of money.

There are several important details to these calculations that should not be overlooked:

1. Be careful to use the yield of the bond and not the coupon rate. If you buy a municipal bond at a discount, its effective yield will be higher than the coupon rate, just as with other bonds. The converse is true for municipals bought at a premium.

2. Do not figure in capital gains if you buy the bond at a discount. Capital gains are subject to federal tax.

3. Be sure to include all the taxes in your tax bracket from which your bond is exempt. For instance, if your state has an income tax from which your bond is exempt, then add that in when figuring your tax bracket. After all, if the interest were from a corporate bond, you would have to pay state taxes on it.

4. Your effective tax bracket for calculations such as this is *not* the tax bracket you are currently paying. It is the bracket in which you would be if your received the interest without its being tax free. This can be important if your income is on the edge of another tax bracket or if you are considering investing a substantial amount in tax-free bonds.

Another thing to watch for is the tax status of the municipal bonds you own within the particular state in which you live. Granted, state tax is far less that federal tax (from which your interest *is* exempt), but the state still takes its chunk. You should determine the total benefits of any financial instrument you are considering for purchase, whether taxable or not. Most states, but not all, exempt their own municipal bonds within that state. Only 15 states exempt the interest from municipal bonds of other states from income tax within their state. Thus if you presently live in one state but are thinking of moving or retiring to another, you should check carefully the tax status of your bonds within the state to which you may move.

Here is a rundown of the status of tax-exempt bonds in all 50 states and the District of Columbia. Keep in mind that *all* are exempt from federal taxes. Also, laws change. No matter what the following chart says, verify the tax status of any municipal bond you are considering with a reputable bond broker.

STATE	STATE'S OWN MUNICIPAL BONDS TAX-EXEMPT WITHIN THAT STATE	MUNICIPAL BONDS OF OTHER STATES TAX-EXEMPT WITHIN THAT STATE
Alabama	x	
Alaska	x	x
Arizona	x	
Arkansas	x	
California	x	
Colorado		
Connecticut	x	x
Delaware	x	
District of Columbia	x	x
Florida	x	x
Georgia	x	
Hawaii	x	
Idaho	x	
Illinois		
Indiana	x	x
Iowa		
Kansas		
Kentucky	x	
Louisiana	x	x
Maine	x	
Maryland	x	
Massachusetts	x	
Michigan	x	
Minnesota	x	
Mississippi	x	
Missouri	x	
Montana	x	
Nebraska	x	x
Nevada	x	x
New Hampshire	x	
New Jersey	x	
New Mexico	x	x
New York	x	
North Carolina	x	
North Dakota	x	
Ohio	x	
Oklahoma		
Oregon	x	
Pennsylvania	x	
Rhode Island	x	
South Carolina	x	
South Dakota	x	x
Tennessee	x	
Texas	x	x
Utah	x	x
Vermont	x	x
Virginia	x	
Washington	x	x
West Virginia	x	
Wisconsin		
Wyoming	x	x

Some cities also have income taxes. Thus you will see in the press mentions of triple tax-exempt bonds, meaning they are exempt from federal, state, and city taxes.

The municipal bond buyer should be aware that there are some taxes from which no municipal bonds are exempt. These are capital gains and inheritance taxes. Capital gains tax is paid, of course, only once, when you sell a bond (if you sell) at a price over what you paid for it. Or it must be paid at maturity if you bought the bond at a discount. Also—retirees beware—the 1983 Social Security Act Amendment states that interest from municipal bonds must be included in the taxpayer's modified adjusted gross income when determining whether benefits under social security are to be taxed.

ARE MUNICIPAL BONDS FOR YOU?

The tax-exempt status of the dollars you receive from municipal bonds should make up for the lower interest rates municipals usually pay. However, your tax bracket must be high enough to make that possible. In the past, municipal bond interest rates were about 30 to 35% lower than interest rates paid by equivalent corporate bonds. The investor would have to have been in the 30 to 35% tax bracket to make up that gap. Better, of course, if he or she were in a higher tax bracket, so that the actual number of dollars the investor could keep would be *greater* than the number that could have been kept if the interest were taxable.

Recently there has been a tendency for tax-free yields to approach more closely the yields of corporate bonds. This has been in response to what is perceived as an increase in risk associated with municipal securities or, at least, with some of the municipalities that issue such securities. But whatever the interest rates municipals pay, whether it is 10% lower or 30% lower than their corporate counterparts, the investor obviously must be in a higher bracket in order to make tax-free bonds worth acquiring.

Municipal bonds also require a higher initial investment than corporate bonds. Generally, the lowest denomination of a tax-free bond is $5,000, compared with $1,000 denominations for corporate bonds.

Safety is also an important factor to the purchaser of municipal bonds. Since such bonds are usually purchased to produce income, the investor doesn't want to monitor them as closely as he or she might watch a stock portfolio. Nevertheless, *all* your investments should be reviewed periodically. While it is assumed that municipalities or municipal authorities are more stable than corporations, it isn't always true.

The most infamous case of municipal bond failure in recent years involved bonds issued by the Washington (State) Public Power Supply System. These unfortunate bonds, known as the Whoops bonds, are virtually worthless because of the failure to complete the nuclear power plants for which they were issued. (Money to meet the interest payments was to have been generated by those plants.) It is hardly comforting to know that these bonds carried a Standard & Poor's A rating for almost five years after they were issued.

Municipal bonds are rated by Moody's MIG (Municipal Investment Grade) and Standard & Poor's. The rating levels are similar to those for corporate bonds (see Chapter Nine). The lowest rating considered investment grade (safe for both individual and institutional investors) is Baa by Moody's and BBB by Standard & Poor's.

TYPES OF MUNICIPAL BONDS

Bonds within a single issue will be known collectively as "term" bonds or "serial" bonds. Term bonds within an issue or segment of an issue all mature on the same date and have the same coupon rate. Serial bonds have different maturities and different coupon rates. The later the maturity date, the higher the coupon rate on the individual bond tends to be.

Municipal bonds have become increasingly complex in recent years. Traditionally, however, they will fall into one of the following categories:

General obligation bonds: These are backed by the full faith and credit of the municipality. They are considered the most secure type of municipal bond, since "full faith and credit" includes the power of taxation with which to generate funds to meet the bond obligations.

Special tax bonds: These are bonds whose backing is limited to a specific tax, such as a sales tax or a specific product.

Revenue bonds: The backing for these bonds is the income from the facility being financed.

ELEVEN

Government Securities

Direct issues of the United States government fall into two broad categories: nonmarketable securities and marketable securities. Nonmarketable securities include special issues to trust funds and foreign central banks; but the best known of the government's marketable securities are the Series E and Series H savings bonds. They can be purchased only from the federal government (although you may do so through your bank), and when they mature you receive all your principal plus all your compounded interest in one lump sum. (That lump sum will be the face value of the bond.) If you wish to sell your bonds before maturity, you send them back to the Treasury (again, perhaps through a bank), and you receive your principal and whatever interest has accrued to date. There is no secondary market for these issues, so you do not sell them on an exchange or to another investor. There is a similarity between savings bonds and shares in mutual funds or money market funds. You do not trade these shares among other investors or brokers either; you buy them from or sell them to the issuer.

Relatively little appears in the financial news about non-negotiable government securities, but you will see a great deal about the other major category, marketable securities. Marketable securities of the United States government constitute the largest securities market of any single issuer in the world. Many brokerages are in existence for the sole purpose of handling transactions in these issues. They fall into the following categories:

1. *Treasury bonds:* These have 10- to 30-year maturities and are available in minimum denominations of $1,000.

The direct issues of the government
consist of bonds, which have the longest
maturities; notes, which have medium-term
maturities; and bills, which have maturities of
one year or less.

Government Security Prices Show Rise

NEW YORK—Bond prices rose
sharply yesterday as investors
snapped up Government
securities in the belief that a
drop in interest rates may be
imminent.

When bond prices rise, their yields drop.
This is because the interest amount, which
never varies, constitutes a smaller percent of
the market price.

When interest rates fall, the prices of
bonds that are already issued rise so that
their yields will fall, thus staying in line with
current rates of interest.

New issues of U.S. Treasury securities are
sold at regularly scheduled auctions.
Seasoned securities are subsequently sold by
government security dealers.

Yields Fall at Treasury Bill Auction

WASHINGTON—The Treasury
sold 7.52 billion of 52-week bills
at an average rate of 7.94%.

That was down from the
8.12% at the previous auction
of 52-week bills held last
month.

The department received
bids totaling $28.73 billion and
accepted those in a range of
7.93% to 7.955% including
$545.72 million in noncompeti-
tive bids. The average price
was 91.972.

Treasury bills, unlike bonds and notes, are
sold at discount. Interest as well as principal
are received only at maturity when the face
amount is given to the investor. The discount
price is set so that receipt of the face value
at maturity will yield the stipulated percent
of interest. The price is quoted as a percent
of par. That is the discount from the face
value at which the bond is sold. The price as
a percent of par is given in the last sentence.

**Dealers in government securities submit
competitive bids.** After the winning bids are
accepted, noncompetitive bids from
individuals are set at the average of the
competitive bids accepted. That way
individuals do not have to compete with
professionals on the bidding, and they are
assured a fair price.

2. *Treasury notes:* These have 1- to 10-year maturities and are
available in minimum denominations of $5,000. Sometimes
they may be bought in $1,000 denominations.

3. *Treasury bills (T-bills):* These have maturities of 1 year or less. They are available in minimum denominations of $10,000.

Most people aren't aware that interest from Treasury bills, bonds, and notes is exempt from state and local income taxes. Such interest is not, however, exempt from federal income taxes.

Only the bills, bonds, and notes listed above are direct (and marketable) obligations of the U.S. Treasury. In the news you will see references to bonds issued by U.S. agencies such as the Government National Mortgage Association (Ginnie Maes) or the Federal Land Bank. While default of any of these agencies is probably unthinkable, their bonds are nevertheless not direct obligations of the government (see the section on U.S. agency bonds later in this chapter).

New issues of Treasury securities are sold at regularly scheduled auctions. The twenty to thirty brokerage firms that deal specifically in government securities submit all the competitive bids except for representatives of some foreign interests. After all the bids are opened, the winning bids are selected and all the noncompetitive bids are pegged at the average of the competitive bids. In the Treasury bill example, the noncompetitive bid price was set in the middle of a 3-point spread (7.93% to 7.95%). With this procedure it is clear that individual investors do not have to compete with professionals. You can submit a bid through a bank or a broker, or you can obtain forms from your nearest Federal Reserve Bank and submit bids directly to the Fed.

QUOTATIONS OF BONDS AND NOTES

Government securities are identified by date and coupon rate. Quotations of bonds and notes are lumped together, since there is in fact no difference between them except that bonds can be issued for a longer maturity. Even so, a seasoned bond could have only three or four years left in it, while a new Treasury note could not mature for up to 10 years. An "n" in the quotations between the maturity date and the rate indicates that the security is a note; otherwise it is a bond.

Government bonds and notes pay interest semiannually. The

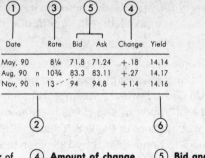

(1) Month and year of maturity

(2) n = Treasury note

(3) Coupon rate the bond is paying on face value

(4) **Amount of change** from the last price of the last trading period; decimals indicate thirty-secondths

(5) **Bid and ask prices** in percent of par except that decimal points are thirty-secondths

(6) **Yield to maturity,** given the last price; given in percent of par

month of maturity is also one of the months that interest is paid; the other payment is six months later. Most are on the fifteenth or at the end of the month.

QUOTATIONS OF U.S. TREASURY BILLS

Treasury bills, or T-bills, as they are called, are different from bonds and notes in that they do not make periodic interest payments. These short-term instruments pay only their face value on maturity, which is always in a year or less.

The bills are sold at an amount less than par (called "at a discount") calculated so that payment *of only the face value* will yield the interest rate designated by the market price. For new bills, noncompetitive bids from individuals must include a check for the face amount of the bond desired. After the price is determined, a refund of the remainder (the difference between the price and the face value) is immediately mailed back to the buyer.

Treasury bills are watched closely, because there is usually a close link between Treasury bill yields and the prime interest rate. T-bills are probably the primary short-term instrument in the United States after certificates of deposit. The market for these instruments is enormous.

. Like bonds and notes, Treasury bills are identified by the maturity date, which incidentally is always a Thursday.

The most distinguishing thing about Treasury bill quotations is that the prices are quoted as a percentage discount from par value. Thus if a $10,000 T-bill maturing in 52 weeks was quoted at 10%, that would mean that the bill was being sold at a 10% discount, making for a price of about $9,000. If the bill were maturing in 26 weeks, then the 10% quotations would mean that the discount would be about $500 (half of the full year discount) and the price of the bill would be about $9,500. Likewise, a three-month bill quoted at 10% would mean that the three-month discount would annualize to $250, so that the price would be about $9,750. In each example the word "about" was used because calculations of the prices of bills sold at discount are complex, and they seldom work out exactly to a round number.

Figuring the yield of a T-bill from the discount price is tricky. As in the above example, if a quotation of 10% meant that the price of the bill was $9,000, it would not mean that the *yield* was 10%, since $1,000 is obviously more than 10% of the amount invested, $9,000. It is, in fact, 11.11%.

QUOTATIONS FOR U.S. TREASURY BILLS

Mat. Date	Bid	Asked	Yield
2-20	7.26	7.22	7.49
2-27	7.25	7.21	7.49
3-6	7.25	7.21	7.50
3-13	7.25	7.21	7.51

①   ②   ③

① **Month and day** of maturity (within the next 52 weeks)

② **Bid and asked prices** stated as a percent of discount from the par value

③ **Yield** stated as annualized percent of asked price

To translate the asked price of a T-bill into dollars and cents, you need to subtract the discount price, annualized for however long the maturity of the bill is, from the face value. Here is the formula for doing just that:

$$\underbrace{\frac{\overbrace{\text{asked price}}^{\substack{\text{In decimals} \\ \text{(not percent)}}} \times \overbrace{\text{days to maturity}}^{\substack{\text{Do not count} \\ \text{the first day}}}}{360} \times \text{par value} = \text{DISCOUNT}}_{}$$

In dollars
and cents

U.S. AGENCY BONDS

The agencies of the U.S. government that issue bonds include the following:

Government National Mortgage Association. "Ginnie Mae" finances residential housing where established funding is inadequate. Minimum investment is usually $25,000, depending on the type of Ginnie Mae purchased. Interest is taxable. These bonds are noncallable and usually liquidate early (approximately 12 years).

Federal National Mortgage Association. Fannie Mae purchases residential mortgages from banks and savings and loans during periods of—and in order to ease—tight credit. Minimum investment is usually $10,000. Bonds are noncallable, and some are convertible into FNMA common stock. Interest is taxable. Technically this is a privately owned corporation, but it is regulated by the Secretary of Housing and Urban Development.

Banks for Cooperatives. These banks make loans to farmers' cooperative associations. Minimum investment is $5,000. Bonds are noncallable, and the interest is exempt from state and local income taxes.

Federal Home Loan Bank. The FHLB regulates and makes loans to savings and loan associations. Minimum investment is $10,000. Bonds are noncallable, and the interest is exempt from state and local income taxes.

Federal Intermediate Credit Bank. The FICB makes loans to banks that loan to agricultural concerns. Minimum investment is $5,000. Recent issues are noncallable. Interest is exempt from state and local income taxes.

Federal Land Banks. These banks make real estate and other loans to farmers. Minimum investment is $1,000. Some bonds are callable. Interest is exempt from state and local income taxes.

TWELVE

Options

In the not-too-distant past, options were thought to constitute the nether regions of investing. They were not listed on exchanges, and their quotations did not appear in the newspapers. People who trafficked in options were thought to be insiders, market manipulators, or riverboat gamblers.

Today, in comparison to new investment products introduced in the 1980s, options seem like tame fare. Nevertheless, the ordinary investing public has never quite taken to them. There are two reasons. One is that most investors do not have a clear idea of what an option is; the second is that options require watching. They are more volatile than stocks and bonds, and so one can't tuck them in a portfolio and just check the prices every three months. People who have options usually keep close tabs on them —or they have a great deal of faith in their broker.

WHAT IS AN OPTION?

Instead of representing actual ownership of something (like a share of a company), an option represents the legal right to engage in a specific purchase or sale at a specific price within a specific period of time. There are two kinds of stock options. One is a right to buy stock; the other is a right to sell stock.

Most of us who have had any experience in real estate are familiar with purchase options. If you are selling a tract of land, someone might offer to buy an option on it—say, the right to buy the land at a certain price from you anytime during the next three months. If you agree to sell the option, at any time during those three months the person who buys the option has the right to

CBOE to List Five New Options

CHICAGO—The Chicago Board Options Exchange announced today that the trading of five new options would begin next month. The . . .

Trading of Options on NYSE Composite Index Begins

NEW YORK—For the first time, brokers on the floor of the New York Stock Exchange will be trading options. Only one, so far. The option is based on the exchange's own composite index. . . .

Options are contracts permitting one to buy or to sell a specific stock at a specific price within a specific amount of time. Options come in two forms: calls and puts. A *call* is a contract permitting one to buy stock at the specified price (called a strike price), and a *put* is a contract permitting one to sell stock at the specified price.

Options are traded on exchanges. The Chicago Board Options Exchange (CBOE) lists the most options, but they are also traded, to a lesser extent, on every major stock exchange.

Options may also be traded on commodities, futures contracts, and even indexes. Here, the option is based on a stock index. An arbitrary monetary value is given to points on the index, and the option is settled in cash.

exercise it and purchase your land. If he or she doesn't exercise the option before the three months are up, then you haven't sold your land. But you can keep the money you were given for the option. By selling the option in the first place, you have calculated that its sale price compensates you for having to turn down any other offers you receive during those three months.

The usual reason real estate options are bought is to keep someone else from getting the property. The usual reason for buying or selling stock options is to make money. Investors do not frequently, for instance, acquire shares through option trading. (There are a few other reasons, such as to defer taxes due on the sale of stock from one tax year to the next, which are too complex to consider here.)

Let us say that the price of stock in XYZ Corporation is $25 a share. Let us also say that you pay someone $200 for the right to purchase 100 shares of that stock from them *at that price* anytime within the next three months. Your expectation is that the price of the stock will go up, and if it goes up enough (more than $2 per share in this example), you stand to make money.

If the price of that stock goes up to $30 within the next three months you can exercise your option, giving the other investor

$2,500 for 100 shares of XYZ. Then you can sell them on the open market for $3,000. Your immediate profit is $500. But remember, you previously paid the other investor $200 for the option, and this must be subtracted from your profit, leaving you $300 (not counting commissions).

But there is a simpler way. Let us say that just before you decide to exercise your option, another investor comes along and, seeing you have a valuable option, offers you $500 for it. It would be far simpler to sell your option to that investor (one transaction) than go through the process of buying the shares of XYZ and then selling them on the open market (which is two transactions). You have only one commission to pay instead of two, and most important, you don't have to put up the $2,500 to make the initial stock purchase. Instead of buying the stock at $2,500 and selling it at $3,000, for a 12% profit ($300, after deducting the cost of the option), you buy an option for $200 and sell it for $500. That's a 150% profit on your investment of $200!

Before going further, we should look carefully at the assumptions we made in this example. First of all, we assumed that the price of the stock went from $25 to $30 in less than three months. If the price had stayed at $25 or had gone down during that time, your option would be worthless (who needs to own the right to buy a stock at $35 per share when it's selling for that or less on the open market?), and your loss would be $200 (the full price of the option) or 100% of your investment.

The overall investment strategy in options is not to double or triple your money. Yes, it is possible to do that or better on single transactions, but the risks are unconscionably high. The usual strategy is to spread your risks out over many carefully selected option contracts so that you have a reasonable chance of *some* winners. You will always have losers, but by cutting your losses early (closing contracts as soon as they go against you) and letting your winners "ride," you can hope for a net gain after the dust settles. Thus, as you can see, this is not a game for the faint-hearted.[1]

---

[1] For the pros there are some schemes where the risk is reduced considerably, but so is the potential for reward. It involves buying and selling combinations of options. They are beyond the scope of this book, but you can get an idea of what some of them are like by looking them up in the Glossary. They have colorful names like "butterfly spread," "straddle," "bull spread," "calendar spread," and "diagonal spread."

CALL OPTIONS

Now, let's get a bit more technical. As we said at the beginning of the chapter, there are two kinds of options. A *call* is a right to buy stock (to "call" it in), and a *put* is a right to sell stock (to "put" it to someone).

Call options are the easiest type to understand. If you see references to options in the newspaper with no further qualifications, then it is likely they are talking about calls. Our option to buy XYZ stock in the first example was a call option. The position of the investor was that he or she thought the price of the stock would go up. The investor bought a call that permitted the purchase of 100 shares of XYZ at $25 within the next three months. (The price at which the option permits you to purchase the stock is the "strike" price or the "exercise" price.)

Call options may also be sold. After all, if you bought a call option, then technically someone had to sell it to you. However, in the purchase or sale of options you never deal with specific individuals. As with most stock transactions, your broker purchases the option for you on an exchange. The main exchange for options is the Chicago Board Options Exchange (CBOE), although most other stock exchanges now list options too. To reverse our earlier example, if you *sold* a call for $200 to buy 100 shares of XYZ within three months for $25 per share, then you would *receive* $200 instead of paying it out. You would have then sold someone else the right to buy those shares *from you*.

Several things can happen now:

1. *The price of the stock does not go up.* Let us say that the shares of XYZ never got above $25; in fact, they fell to $23. Why would anyone exercise an option to buy the shares from you for $25 per share when they could buy them on the open market for $23 per share? The other investor, whoever it was, took a chance that the stock would go up. It didn't, he or she never exercised the option, and lost $200. You, on the other hand, evidently thought the stock would not go up, and you were right. You made $200.

2. *The price of the stock goes up.* Whenever the market price of a stock rises above the designated strike price (in our example, the strike price is $25), then you are in danger of the option being

exercised. When an option moves against you (in this case, if the market price of the underlying stock has risen above the strike price of the call you sold), the easiest thing to do is to "bail out." You can terminate your obligations under any options contract by buying or selling an option with the same contract specifications. This is not selling the original contract—it is canceling one contract by another. If you sell a call, you get out of it—cancel it out —by buying a call with the same terms. Likewise, if you buy a call you can close it by selling a call with the same terms. In options, this is called a "closing transaction."

In our example, the initial transaction was the sale of a call for $200 giving another person the right to buy 100 shares of XYZ at $25 a share from the person selling the call. Since the market price of XYZ has risen above the strike price of $25, the investor selling the call could terminate the contract by buying another call with exactly the same terms. Unfortunately, since the right to buy the stock at $25 per share is more valuable now, the closing transaction (the purchase of the call) will cost more than the amount the investor received from the purchaser of the first option. The investor thus has the choice of losing a few hundred dollars in the purchase of the now more expensive option in the closing transaction, or selling the stock itself if the option is exercised (which eventually it will be, as long as its market price is above the strike price).

Selling the stock, if the option is exercised, is not a disaster. The buyer (the one exercising the option) must pay the strike price ($25 per share) to the investor who sold the call, so that the investor selling the stock still comes out with $200 more (the amount paid for the option) than he or she had in the beginning. The original position was XYZ stock worth $2,500; the final position is $2,700 ($2,500 received for the XYZ stock and $200 received for the option). What is lost to the first investor is the full increase in the value of the stock that resulted from the rise in its price. That investor gave up the opportunity to earn that extra money in order to guarantee a $200 profit (the price he got for selling the option), and to eliminate the possibility of a loss (no matter how low the price of the stock fell during those three months, the investor could always sell it at $25 per share). This is called a "covered option," and will be discussed later.

Without going further into the complexities of calls, there are important conformities to which all option contracts adhere that were not mentioned in the previous discussion:

1. The strike prices of the stocks that options are written on are $5 apart ($25, $30, $35) so long as the strike price is below $50 per share. If it is above, the increment is $10.

2. Options are created (or "written") for 3-month, 6-month, and 9-month durations. The last day for trading options is the third Friday of the month in which they expire. In our example, XYZ options might expire in January, April, and July; or perhaps in February, May, and August. When you buy an option, it might not have exactly 3, 6, or 9 months left to run. For example, if you wanted to buy an option on XYZ, you would look in the newspaper to see on what 3-month cycle XYZ options were written. If they are on the January, April, July cycle and it is December, then you have a choice of one, four, and seven months.

3. All options give holders the right to purchase or sell 100 shares. If more shares are required (in multiples of 100), more option contracts must be bought.

The point of the standardization of strike prices, expiration dates, and share amounts is to provide liquidity in the options market. Liquidity is important unless the original purchaser of an option always plans to exercise it. In fact, liquidity is vital because most options are closed out before they are exercised. If you had purchased an option for XYZ at a strike price of $23.50 per share expiring on May 6, you might have a hard time selling that option if you wanted to do so. Who else would want an option with those exact specifications, and how would you find that person? On the other hand, if you had a "standard" option with a strike price of $20 per share expiring on the third Friday of April (or $25 per share expiring on the third Friday in May), your option would have the same contractual components as many other options. This means that all can be traded freely, and that means liquidity. Thus, if you decide you want to buy options, you look in the paper to see what is available with respect to strike price, expiration date, and cost, and you can be assured that whenever you wish to close your option contracts by buying or selling (whichever is appropriate), you will have no trouble doing so.

Perhaps a word should be said here about the price of options. Do not confuse the cost of the option with the strike price. The strike price is a stipulation in the option contract and has to do only with the price at which you are guaranteed that you may purchase or sell shares. The price of the option, called a "premium," is up to the market and depends on a number of variables. For instance, if you price an option for XYZ at a strike price of $25, and the price of XYZ is already $30 a share, then obviously the option is worth (the premium will be) at least $500. If, in addition, the option has six more months, then the time left in the option is also worth money. After all, the stock could go up some more: let's add another $250 to the option price. And finally, if traders think very highly of that stock and *expect* it to go up soon, then the price of the option will go even higher. In short, you could end up paying over a thousand dollars for such an option. More typically, however, options are much cheaper. Many, as you will see, are priced under $100.

PUT OPTION

Puts are the opposite of calls. They are the right to *sell* stock at a specific price and within a specified time limit. Thus, if you buy a put with the same terms as our original XYZ option, you have the right to sell someone XYZ at $25 per share. That will be worth a good deal of money if the price of XYZ drops to $15 a share; in fact, it would be worth over $1,000. You don't even have to own the stock. What you would probably do is close out your put option by selling a put with the same contract stipulations. Such an option would be worth, as we said, over $1,000. Subtract from that the price you paid for the put and the option commission, and you still have a tidy profit.

If you sell a put, then you have sold someone else the right to "put" XYZ to you at the stipulated price. If the market price of XYZ stays above the exercise price, the option will not be exercised (why would someone insist on selling you XYZ at $25 when they could sell it on the open market for more), and you simply keep the amount you received from the original sale of the option.

There are several things to keep in mind about options. First of all, the owners of options do not own the underlying stock. They cannot vote at stockholder meetings or receive dividends. There is only an agreement that the holder (the investor who has purchased an option) has a right to buy stock by exercising the option and paying the strike (if it is a call) or a right to sell stock and receive the strike price (if it is a put).

Second, an option is a wasting asset. That is, its value decreases with time and (in the case of options) eventually disappears altogether. For example, if XYZ stock is selling at 27, a call with a strike price of $25 for XYZ is automatically worth $200, since one could exercise the option, buy the stock at 25, and resell it at 27. (An option with automatic value is said to be "in the money.") If the option didn't expire for six months, then the extra time the option had to run would be worth something. But the closer the option gets to its expiration date, the closer its price approaches zero (if the option is not in the money) or its automatic value (if the option is in the money).

Another point to keep in mind is that listed options are not available on every stock. Exchanges that trade options agree among themselves as to what stock options will be offered, and on which exchanges they will be listed. As far as which exchange lists which option, the exchanges actually decide that by lottery. Also, the exchanges that list the underlying stock do not (or at least rarely) list the option on that stock too. As you would expect, options are available for many issues listed on the New York Stock Exchange, but only for a few over-the-counter securities.

A conservative use of options that many brokers recommend is writing "covered" options. A covered option is an option written on a quantity of stock which the investor owns. For example, if you sold a call on XYZ (sold someone else the right to buy XYZ from you) and you had XYZ in your portfolio, that is a "covered" call. If the option is exercised, you could provide the stock at once from your portfolio. This is a conservative way to make extra income, since if the option is not exercised, you have the money you were paid for the call. If it *is* exercised, you get the strike price for the stock (which should be slightly higher than the market price at the time you sold the call) and you still have the money you received for the call. Either way, you end up with more than you started. If the stock price moves up and you feel strongly about retaining the stock, you can buy a closing call and keep from relinquishing the shares. You will be out the price of a call, but you will be compensated by holding more valuable stock. As mentioned earlier, this is a "no lose—limited win" way of protecting the value of your portfolio.[2]

To summarize our discussion of options, the components of an option are these:

1. Name (of the underlying security)

2. Type (call or put)

3. Strike price (or exercise price) at which one can buy or sell the underlying stock

4. Expiration month (the actual day is the third Friday of the month)

If you *buy* an option as an opening transaction (not in combination with other previously bought or sold options) you will eventually do one of three things:

1. *Exercise it* if it is to your advantage to do so. You simply inform your broker. If you are exercising a call, you will pay the strike price for the stock plus a commission to your broker for the purchase.

2. *Terminate it* with a closing transaction (a sale of an option with the same contract specifications). This is the most likely course of action. If you can sell it for more than you paid for it (this assumes the price of the underlying stock has moved in the direction you want it to), you have made a profit. You will also, of course, have to figure in the commission for the two option transactions, (the purchase and the sale). Option commissions are, however, generally quite low.

3. *Let it expire.* If there is nothing to be gained by items 1 or 2, you can let the option expire. However, it is almost always best to close the initial purchase of an option by selling an

[2]A detailed discussion of options is beyond the scope of this book. For a detailed treatment, see my *The Investor's Guide to Stock Quotations,* published by Harper & Row.

option. Even if you get far less than you paid for the initial option, you are recovering at least a part of your loss.

If you *sell* an option as an opening transaction (not in connection with other options), one of these things will happen:

1. It will be *exercised by the purchaser,* and you must fulfill your obligation under the terms of the option. You have no way of knowing when an option you sold will be exercised. If, for instance, 5,000 options with your contract specifications are exercised in one day, the Options Clearing Corporation doles out the exercises to sellers of the option (actually, to their brokers) on a random basis. Once you are informed, it is too late to close your contract by buying a contract. You deliver the stock from your account, if you have it, or buy the stock on the open market and deliver it if you don't. Another choice you might have is to deliver short. This means you borrow the stock from your broker to fulfill the delivery. You have to have a margin (credit) account with your broker to do this. Also, don't forget that having an option exercised is not a tragedy. You receive the strike price for the stock, and you also have the price you received (the "premium") when you originally sold the option.

2. You will *terminate the option* by purchasing a closing option of the same contract specifications. The difference between the cost of this transaction and the premium you received when you originally sold the option will be your profit. If the cost of this transaction exceeds that of the original option (as it will if the stock moves against you), the difference will be your loss.

3. The option will expire (as explained earlier in the chapter), and you will keep the entire premium you received from the original sale. Note that this will not happen if the option is "in the money" even a fraction of a point.

OPTION QUOTATIONS

Because of the complexity of options, we saved the quotation example for last.

Note that the example is in the format frequently used for daily listings in the newspapers. Although Sunday papers and other weekly papers typically use a different format, the data are the same, so that if you can read the example, you can read a weekly listing too. Added to the weekly listings may be the number of options traded in the week and the number of "open interest" contracts—that is, the number of contracts that have yet to be closed.

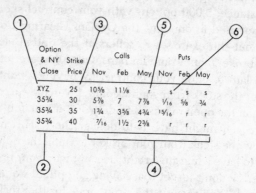

Option & NY Close	Strike Price	Calls Nov	Feb	May	Puts Nov	Feb	May
XYZ	25	10⅝	11⅛	r	s	s	s
35¾	30	5⅞	7	7⅞	1/16	⅝	¾
35¾	35	1¾	3⅝	4¾	15/16	r	r
35¾	40	7/16	1½	2⅜	r	r	r

① **Name of the option** (that is, the issuing company).

② **Closing price** of underlying stock on the New York Stock Exchange (previous day). New York close is not given on first line entry.

③ **Strike price** at which the underlying stock can be bought or sold.

④ **Prices or "premiums" of options** shown in points (as in stock quotations).

⑤ **"r" means option did not trade** during the period reported. (Some other symbol may be used.)

⑥ **"s" means an option** with those specifications was not offered for sale as of the reporting date. (Some other symbol may be used.)

THIRTEEN

Futures Contracts

There are three types of futures contracts: commodity futures, financial futures, and index futures. The primary example of the latter is the new stock index futures whose consideration we will put off until the next chapter. Here we deal only with commodity and financial futures.

A futures contract for a commodity is an agreement to deliver a certain quantity of that commodity. The contract specifies the time of delivery (usually a month), the quality of the commodity, and the price to be paid.

A futures contract for a financial instrument, usually called a "financial future," is the same except that the "commodity" being delivered is a collection of financial instruments like Treasury bills (say, a million dollars worth) or French francs.

Certain characteristics are necessary for items on which futures are traded. There must be sufficient supply and demand to make a liquid market. The commodity must be divisible into standard units, like ounces or barrels or francs. Also, the commodity must be gradable. This last requirement is not applicable to a commodity like a foreign currency, but it is very important for any physical resource like oil or an agricultural commodity.

About 98% of all futures contracts never result in delivery. Before the delivery date arrives, a closing contract is usually obtained. Futures contracts thus change hands many times.

There is a great deal of similarity between futures contracts and options. One is that both are highly leveraged instruments: With a relatively low investment, you can control large amounts of a commodity. There is an important difference, however: Futures are not a "wasting asset." In the options chapter it was explained that the closer an options contract gets to expiration the less valuable it becomes, and when it expires there are no consequences except that it become functionless and therefore valueless. A futures contract, however, does not expire. When it matures, it requires delivery. If you are trading futures as a speculator, there is no need to worry about delivery; speculators never accept delivery of a physical commodity. Your broker will warn you well in advance of coming delivery dates and make sure you close out your position with an offsetting contract.

In newspaper articles about futures contracts you will see references to speculators and to hedgers. A "hedger" is a person who either produces or utilizes a commodity. Such an individual would buy a futures contract to lock in a price for a certain amount of a commodity he or she needs to conduct business. A "speculator" is a person who is willing to assume the risks the hedger is trying to avoid. For taking these risks, the speculator expects the potential of high profits. The presence of speculators is absolutely necessary for a liquid and balanced market; otherwise there would be no one for hedgers to buy or sell their contracts to or from.

Like options, one can either buy or sell futures contracts. If you buy a futures contract you are buying a delivery, and should you hold the contract until maturity, you would accept delivery and pay the specified price. Buying a futures contract is called "going long." If you sell a futures contract, you are "going short." You are obligated to make a delivery of the specified amount and quality, and to receive the stipulated payment.

Also like options, a futures contract is offset by buying or selling a like contract. The *purchase* of a contract to deliver 25,000 pounds of copper on a certain date is offset by the *sale* of a contract to deliver 25,000 pounds of copper on the same date.

COMMODITY QUOTATIONS

To determine the price of each contract, multiply the unit price by the contract size. The contract size is usually stated after the name of the commodity. In the example here, you see first the name of the contract (silver) followed by the contract size (5,000 troy ounces). Next shown is the manner of pricing, cents per troy ounce. Note that the prices are in cents, as stated, not dollars. Thus the high of the March contract is 803.5 cents, which is $8.035 per troy ounce, not $803.50 per ounce. That figure, times the contract size, 5,000, makes for a price of $40,175 per contract. The speculator will only have to put up from 5 to 10% of that figure, or whatever percentage is required by his or her broker or the exchange.

COMMODITY FUTURES QUOTATION

				Net	Season's Range	
	High	Low	Close	Chg.	High	Low
Feb	795.0	785.0	794.5	+7.5	1500.0	775.0
Mar	803.5	795.0	803.5	+7.5	1500.0	777.0
Apr	812.0	802.0	812.0	+7.5	1530.0	794.5
Jun	833.0	823.0	831.5	+7.5	1565.0	812.0
Aug	851.0	845.0	851.0	+7.5	1470.0	837.0

SILVER, 5,000 troy oz.; cents per troy oz.

(1) **Contract size**

(2) **Manner of pricing**

(3) **Contract price** in cents per troy ounce (to calculate the price, multiply the price times the contract size

(4) **Month of delivery**

(5) **Change** from previous close (in cents)

FINANCIAL FUTURES

There is little difference between financial futures and commodity futures. There are hedgers and speculators just as in physical commodities. In this case, the hedgers need the financial instruments, or they need to lock in specific interest rates. Financial futures are written on fixed-rate instruments such as Treasury bonds and certificates of deposit, or fixed amounts of foreign currencies. It is the fixed-rate component with which hedgers seek to protect themselves against loss and with which speculators seek to make profits. (With currencies it is the exchange rate, which we will not go into here.) This is possible because the price at which fixed-rate instruments may be bought or sold has an inverse relationship to the movement of interest rates. As interest rates move up, the resale value of a fixed-rate instrument, which has already been issued, moves down; and as interest rates fall, its resale value rises. Financial futures are based on this simple relationship. (For a more detailed description of the relationship of interest rates to fixed income securities, see Chapter Nine.)

By taking long or short positions in futures, portfolio managers, corporate treasurers, and financial planners seek to protect their investments or future investments against adverse interest rate movements or changes in foreign currency rates. Thus, hedgers play the same role in financial futures as they do in commodity futures. For instance, a portfolio manager might anticipate falling interest rates just before a large number of CDs become due. By purchasing CD futures, the manager could guarantee a currently profitable rate of return when it is time for the funds from the CDs to be reinvested, no matter what has happened to interest rates in the meantime. Likewise, a larger manufacturer who purchases electronic components abroad might hedge against a future unfavorable currency exchange rate by buying currency futures. Thus, for the hedger, financial futures are a kind of insurance.

TREASURY BILLS—$1 MILLION; PTS OF 100%

	Open	High	Low	Settle	Chg.	Discount Settle	Chg.	Open Intrst
Mar	86.34	86.42	86.11	86.14	−.08	13.86	+.08	14,670
June	86.49	86.57	86.28	86.30	−.09	13.70	+.09	10,445
Sept	86.65	86.69	86.41	86.44	−.08	13.65	+.08	4,168
Dec	86.67	86.77	86.50	86.51	−.11	13.49	+.11	2,042

(1) Size of contract.

(2) Manner in which price is quoted.

(3) Month of delivery.

(4) Prices are in percent of face value.

(5) Prices are also shown as percent of discount from face value.

FOURTEEN

Stock Index Futures

The 1980s has seen the commercial introduction of more new financial instruments (often called "financial products") than in the whole 200-year history of investing in the United States. Stock index futures are the newest among them, and they can be difficult to understand. So before attempting an explanation, we will review the basics of a futures contract.

A futures contract is a contract to buy or to sell a specific product or commodity at a predetermined price and at a predetermined time in the future. In the case of a stock index future, the "product" or "commodity" is something quite intangible: the numerical value of an index. That numerical value also has a dollar equivalent which is assigned to the index. For instance, one point on the index could equal $100.

The investor need not own any of the stocks that make up the index. When a contract matures, the investor who still has an open contract pays or takes receipt of the amount of money at which the index is valued. Nothing changes hands except cash. There is no delivery of a portfolio of securities.

Many stock index futures are based on long-established indexes originally designed to measure the total market performance of a specific group of securities. The Major Market Index, however, is an example of an index that was created especially for the purpose of assigning a futures contract to it. The Major Market Index is compiled and published by the Chicago Board of Trade, the major futures trading exchange.

There has been a great deal of interest in establishing a stock index future on the most popular index average of all, the Dow

Jones industrial average (DJIA). However, the Dow Jones Company, which owns the DJIA, has managed to block all attempts to base futures on this indicator. Its concern is that the integrity of the average might be compromised, and that futures, because of traders' expectations, might begin to assert some kind of influence over the index itself—or rather, the market prices of the stocks contained in the index. There has been evidence that this has happened to other indexes on which futures have been based, although so far to a relatively small degree.

Stock index futures have been developed for all of the other major indexes. The most well known are these:

1. NYSE Composite Index, made up of all common stocks traded on the New York Stock Exchange

2. S & P Composite Index (known also as the S & P 500 index), made up of Standard & Poor's selection of 500 stocks traded on the NYSE, AMEX, and OTC

3. *Value Line* Composite Index, made up of *Value Line*'s selection of 1,700 stocks traded on the NYSE, AMEX, regional, and OTC markets

4. Major Market Index, made up of 20 blue-chip stocks whose options are traded on the Chicago Board of Trade

By means of a stock index future, an investor can participate in the overall performance of a market as represented by the stock index future. No one stock makes or breaks the performance of the index. The investor using stock index futures contracts feels he or she can anticipate market moves but doesn't wish to pinpoint specific stocks that will perform according to prediction, as would have to be done with a usual stock portfolio.

In all but the *Value Line* index, the individual stocks that make up the index are weighted to reflect the number of shares outstanding in each issue. In the *Value Line* index, all stocks are rated equally. Weighting a stock means that the influence of that stock on the overall index is greater than other stocks, or that it is adjusted in some way in relation to other stocks because it has more shares outstanding, or is more expensive, or is in some way more important.

Stocks within most indexes are weighted according to the

number of shares outstanding because a rise in the security price of a company with a large number of shares outstanding creates more equity dollars than the same increase in the price of shares of a company with fewer shares outstanding. For instance, if the stock of a company with 10 million shares outstanding rises by 1 dollar, 10 million equity dollars are created, whereas if the same price increase occurred for the stock of a company with 1 million shares outstanding, only 1 million dollars in equity is created.

As an example of how stock index contracts work, we will describe the New York Stock Exchange futures contract, which is based on the NYSE Composite Index. The monetary value assigned to the index is $500 times the number at which the index stands. Thus if the index were at 100, the dollar value would be $50,000. If the index rose one-half point (to 100.5), the value would be $50,250. When we consider the quotations for stock index futures, you will see that they are priced according to the same system. Thus while the index may stand at 100 ($50,000), the market price of the six-month contract could be any price. It might, for instance, be 100.60 ($50,300), or 101.2 ($50,600), or 101.7 ($50,850). In the following discussion be sure to keep in mind the difference between the value of the index itself and the market prices of the futures contracts.

Future contracts on the NYSE Composite Index are available for 3 months, 6 months, and 9 months. As one contract matures, a new 9-month contract is introduced. NYSE futures are on a March, June, September, and December cycle.

The market price you will pay for a futures contract depends on a number of factors:

1. The current monetary value of the Composite Index ($500 per point).
2. The estimation of the marketplace—that is, other traders—as to the future of the market. Will it go up or down, and by how much?
3. The length of the contract. Obviously, a contract with 6 months left would bring a higher price than a contract for 3 months, since the former would have a longer time to anticipate the desired market movement.

If the NYSE index closed at 108.75, the dollar value of the index itself on that day would be $54,375. Typical contract prices for futures contracts on that day might be something like those shown in the example below:

On a day that the index stands at 108.75 ($54,375):
The 3-month contract might be priced at 111.55 ($55,775).
The 6-month contract might be priced at 113.55 ($56,775).
The 9-month contract might be priced at 115.55 ($57,775).

Note that in the example, for a 3-month contract investors will pay (if they are buying) or receive (if they are selling) a $1,400 premium above "spot" (the current price). For each additional three months, in the 6-month or 9-month contracts, traders are paying (or receiving) an additional $1,000. Such a spread between the current level of the index and the 3-month, 6-month, and 9-month contracts represents an amount the market might rise or fall.

Although the index itself moves in increments of one hundredth (.01), the smallest movement allowed for the futures contract is five hundredths (.05), which is known as a "tick." One tick, therefore, has a value of $25.

The minimum margin necessary to purchase a contract is set by the exchange and currently stands at $3,500. (Thus, one doesn't have to pay over $50,000 for a contract!) Profits and losses from futures contracts are credited or debited to investors' accounts every day at the close of trading. If a contract increases in value the profit can be removed from the account and, conversely, if the value of the contract falls, the investor will be called to deposit additional funds should the level drop below "maintenance," which is currently set at $1,500. Since the initial investment per contract can be as low as $3,500, and since the index value can obviously fall more than that amount, it should be clear to any investor considering futures that they have the potential to lose even more money than they initially invested.

The strategy of investors who are bullish on the market is to buy contracts. If the value of the index rises, then the value of the futures contracts rises as if the investor had the same amount of money invested in the underlying stocks. When the investor closes his or her position by selling a like contract, the additional amount received, above what was paid for the initial contract, constitutes the profit (after commissions).

If the market goes against you, contracts may be closed at any time by purchasing or selling the same contract (just as with options), whichever is appropriate. Likewise, if the market has gone in the direction you anticipated and you think it will go no farther, you should close out your position. If a contract is held until maturity, the settlement price is a bit complicated. It is not the closing price on the last day of trading, as one would expect, but the *difference* between that price and the previous day's close.

QUOTATIONS OF STOCK INDEX FUTURES

Futures contracts are priced in points, the same as the index is. The first thing to look for in a quotation is the number of dollars assigned per point. You will usually see this amount given after the name of the contract itself. In the example quotation, you can see that the number is given in the first line; the contracts are priced at $500 per point.

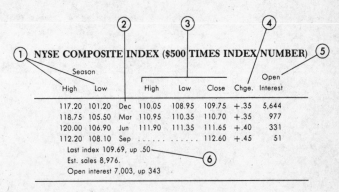

Season						Open
High	Low		High	Low	Close	Chge.	Interest

Season High	Season Low		High	Low	Close	Chge.	Open Interest
117.20	101.20	Dec	110.05	108.95	109.75	+.35	5,644
118.75	105.50	Mar	110.95	110.35	110.70	+.35	977
120.00	106.90	Jun	111.90	111.35	111.65	+.40	331
112.20	108.10	Sep	. . . . . .	. . . . . .	112.60	+.45	51

Last index 109.69, up .50
Est. sales 8,976.
Open interest 7,003, up 343

NYSE COMPOSITE INDEX ($500 TIMES INDEX NUMBER)

① **High and low prices** since the contract began trading

② **Month** in which the contract matures

③ **Prices** during the trading period covered

④ **Change** in price from the close of the previous trading period

⑤ **Number of contracts** not closed

⑥ **Present level** of the index

The next thing to look for is where the index stands at present. This is often shown at the end of the quotation. In the example, you can see that the index closed at 109.75. That amount times $500 makes the monetary value of the index $54,875.

Open interest, also shown at the bottom of the quotation, refers to the number of contracts that are outstanding (that have not been closed out). The contracts themselves are distinguished by their month of delivery. The NYSE Composite Index futures contract is on a December, March, June, and September cycle.

Note that the change column shows the change in price for that particular contract from the previous closing price of the same contract. It does not show the change from the close of the Composite Index itself. That may be given in a quotation such as the "Last index" line at the bottom of the example, where it specifies that the 109.69 figure is up .50 from the previous day's index value.

FIFTEEN

Leading Economic Indicators and the GNP

The Index of Leading Economic Indicators is one of three indexes published monthly by the U.S. Department of Commerce. The other two are the Index of Coincident Economic Indicators and the Index of Lagging Economic Indicators. The word "leading" does not mean that the index is more important than the others; it is used in the sense of predicting the direction of economic movement.

The coincident and the lagging indicators, to be discussed later, are given nowhere near the media attention of the leading indicators because most investors, as well as the general public, want to know what's *going* to happen to the economy, not what is happening at the same time (coincident) or after the fact (lagging).

THE PURPOSE OF THE LEADING INDICATORS

The reason the Commerce Department selected certain indicators over others for the leading index was because it was felt these particular indexes were the first to signal forthcoming changes in the economy. Also, reliable data were thought to be available frequently enough to issue meaningful reports on a monthly basis. The indicators are comprehensive and represent a cross section of economic activity in the country.

It was originally hoped that the reliability of the figures would be such that significant revisions would be unnecessary. Unfortunately, they are now subject to seven routine revisions, some of which have occasionally been drastic enough to reverse the direc-

**Leading Economic
Indicator Rises 2.5%**

WASHINGTON—The govern-
ment's index of leading economic indicators rose 2.5 percent in March, the Commerce
Department said today.
    Economists said the jump,
the largest in a year, was a
strong indication that a recovery is under way in the United
States. . . .

Index of Leading Economic Indicators: an
index made up of data from a number of
sectors that reflect the general economy.
Included are the unemployment rate, new
business startups, factory orders, and the
money supply.

The index is released every month by the
Department of Commerce and designed to
forecast economic trends by as much as six
months to a year. A rise in the index for
several months indicates an improving
economy, while several months' drop
indicates a faltering economy.

**Gross National Product
Rises 2.8% in the First
Quarter**

WASHINGTON—The Com-
merce Department reported
yesterday that the U.S. economy rose by 2.8% in the first
quarter of the year.
    This preliminary estimate
of the real gross national product was . . .

Gross national product (GNP): the value
of the output of all goods and services in the
United States in a one-year period. The
figures are released quarterly by the U.S.
Department of Commerce and seasonally
adjusted to an average annual rate.

Real GNP means that the monetary figures
have been adjusted for inflation.

tion of the index. Also, recalculations of past indexes, because of
the addition or deletion of some components, have caused even
more revisions. Recalculations of past index figures are usually an
attempt to further refine the index's predictive capabilities, but
it has also been observed that they can be politically helpful in
demonstrating the effectiveness of the policies of a current ad-
ministration. Nevertheless, on the whole, the Index of Leading
Economic Indicators remains one of the most useful and accurate
predictors of the economic health of the country.

Individual monthly reports from the index are not as significant as their cumulative direction. A rise or fall for one month or
two is not taken seriously unless it is particularly large. An average
rise over many months indicates that the ingredients are in place
for a robust, expanding economy; many months' decline predicts
a shrinking economy. In either case, the important picture is over
the long run.

The individual indicators fall into four broad categories: consumer spending; business investment in equipment, structures, and housing; the balance of exports and imports; and the net purchase of goods and services by federal, state, and local governments. The indicators are listed below. All measure activity from a base value of 100 percent from the year 1967. Some categories use inflation-adjusted dollars, some use current dollars, and some use nonmonetary units like hours or numbers of persons. Results are always given in percentages.

Components of the Index of Leading Economic Indicators

Average workweek for industrial workers

New claims for state unemployment insurance

New orders for consumer goods

Companies receiving slower deliveries from vendors

Net new business formations

Industry orders for new equipment

New building permits

Net changes in inventories

Crude materials prices

Changes in consumer and business credit outstanding

Stock prices (500 common stock issues)

Money supply (M2)

The Index of Leading Economic Indicators was designed to forecast economic trends. As mentioned before, its components are subject to revision. For instance, petroleum and natural gas prices were found to distort the data from crude materials prices and were subsequently dropped from that category. At the same time, installations of telephone trunk lines was added to the new business formations category.

In the past, the index has been fairly good at anticipating recoveries, but it has had less success at predicting recessions. It also, for better or for worse, has had a strong effect on government policy. The avoidance of recessions and excessive inflation can be very important to political careers.

Occasionally you will see reference to the leading economic indicators' sister indexes, the coincident economic indicators and the lagging economic indicators. Economists look to these indexes for confirmation of what was predicted by the leading indicators and even, in retrospect, to determine more accurately when a trend, recession, or recovery began.

Components of the coincident economic indicators include such things as personal income, trade sales, retail sales, and non-agricultural employment. The lagging indicators include book value of trade inventories, business loans outstanding, bank rates on short-term loans, and other indicators expected to be the last to respond to changes in the economy.

THE GROSS NATIONAL PRODUCT (GNP)

The gross national product measures the market value of the final output of all goods and services in a given year. It is the broadest single measure of economic activity in the United States and indicates the health of the national economy. As such, it receives wide attention in the financial news. Figures are released quarterly by the U.S. Department of Commerce. Before the three months of the quarter are ended, there is usually a preliminary report giving a rough estimate of what the figures are expected to be. The actual report comes about three weeks following the close of the quarter.

The percent is always annualized, so that if it is a first quarter report of 2.8% growth, as in our example, the economy would have to continue to grow at exactly the same rate for the remaining three quarters in order for the GNP to be 2.8% for the entire year.

When you see a reference to "real" GNP, it means that the figures have been adjusted for inflation. This is important in comparing present economic conditions with the economy of previous years. It also means you don't have to worry about how much of the GNP is growth and how much is simply the result of inflation. If the GNP is reported before adjustment for inflation, it is called a "nominal" GNP. Obviously, it will be much higher than the real GNP.

One of the challenges of establishing reliable figures for the GNP is to avoid counting the same items twice or three times. Consider, for instance, automobile carburetors. While automobiles are counted in the GNP because they are "final outputs," carburetors are not. Even though the carburetors for many cars are made at an entirely separate factory and may, in fact, be the sole output of that factory, only those carburetors sold to garages will be counted in the GNP. The same situation is true for an item like bread. The wheat from the granary and the flour from the mill are not counted. The value of all these products and processing is reflected in the value of the finished product.

CONSUMER PRICE INDEX (CPI)

The Consumer Price Index is one of the more down-to-earth measures of inflation. It measures the change in the price of a fixed "basket" of 385 goods and services that are selected for their effect on the majority of consumers in the country. Included are such things as food, housing, transportation, fuel, medical care, personal care, and entertainment. Unlike the gross national product, the Consumer Price Index is a measure of inflation, and as the name implies, consumer-oriented. Also, the figures for the CPI are "seasonably adjusted" so that regular periods of low or high buying (like the Christmas season) do not create distortions.

The targeted items are priced in 85 urban centers. Data are collected from department stores, gas stations, and other places of business. Sometimes data are collected from interviews such as those necessary to obtain rental data from 18,000 renters.

The items in the index are weighted, with the cost of rent the most important. Transportation is next, and food and beverage is a close third.

There are two Consumer Price Indexes, but the one you see reported in the media is usually the Consumer Price Index for All Urban consumers (C.P.I.-U). It reflects a wider coverage of the general population, including people with high incomes, retirees, and people on welfare. The other index, the Consumer Price Index for Urban Wage Earners and Clerical Workers (C.P.I.-W) is considerably narrower. It is estimated that while the C.P.I.-U represents 80% of the population, the C.P.I.-W represents only 40%. The C.P.I.-W, which has a large component for mortgages (as opposed to rentals), is important because some automatic cost-of-living increases are tied to it.

UNEMPLOYMENT RATES

Statistics on the unemployment rate are issued the first Friday of every month for the previous month. The data come from household surveys which attempt to represent the size of the civilian workforce, as well as the number of people who are working and not working. It is made up of interviews that canvass 60,000 households and attempts to account for the employment status of all individuals in those families 16 years of age and older. Note that this is a very different approach from the unemployment index that is a component of the Index of Leading Economic Indicators. (It reports only the number of new applications for state unemployment insurance benefits.)

The survey defines an unemployed person as an individual within the stipulated age bracket who did not work during the specific week in the previous month that the survey was made and who attempted to obtain work during the previous four weeks by applying for jobs or registering with unemployment agencies. There are also other restrictions that limit the number of individuals who may be counted as unemployed. However, an attempt has been made to represent workers at all levels of the economy.

The major criticism of the unemployment rate is that the definitions used for the unemployed exclude the discouraged and the hard-core unemployed, as well as part-time workers who are attempting to find full-time work. The discouraged unemployed refers to those no longer seeking work. The hard-core unemployed refers to workers, usually skilled, in professions where there are special circumstances like massive layoffs at an automobile plant, and there are no other jobs in the same area at an equivalent or near equivalent rate of pay. Inclusion of both categories would probably raise the unemployment rate from 2 to 4 percentage points.

The unemployment rate is a powerful leading indicator. No indicator is infallible, but there have been times when it was the only one that signaled a recession was not over, or that one was about to begin—and was right. When the various leading indicators are mixed, many analysts look to the unemployment rate as being the most important.

HOUSING STARTS

Housing starts is followed by many economists and regularly reported in the financial news. The figures are issued monthly by the Bureau of Census and represent the annual rate of startups of privately owned housing units. There is an annual rate for single-family housing units, buildings with two units, three or four units, and five or more units. A startup is interpreted to mean the breaking of ground.

When an economy is going to take a downturn, the housing sector is the first to decline. For that reason, it is regarded as a key leading indicator.

SHORT INTEREST RATIO

Before discussing the short interest ratio, a word should be said about short selling. It is a technique whereby an investor hopes to make money from a drop in the price of a stock. The investor borrows shares from a broker and sells them in the open market. The hope is that the share price will decline. If the price does decline, the investor buys back the same number of shares on the open market and returns them to his or her broker. Let us say the investor sold the borrowed shares for $40 per share. If they were bought back (to return to the broker) two months later at $32 a share, a gross profit of $8 per share has been made. The net profit is determined after deducting commissions for both the sale and the purchase, as well as the interest charged by the brokerage for the loan of the stock.

Several things should be obvious about a short sale. One is that the investor is bearish on the stock (assuming the short sale is not connected with some other investment like options or an arbitrage). The other is that future purchases are now assured, since the investor must eventually buy the same amount of shares again in order to repay the broker.

The New York Stock Exchange and the American Stock Exchange report the outstanding short interest on their exchanges four days after the fifteenth of every month. Short "interest" is defined as the total number of shares sold which were borrowed from brokerage and which have not been repurchased (called "covering") and returned to the broker. The exchange can do this because all transactions involved in shorting, whether it is an initial sale or a covering purchase, must be reported as such at the time of the transaction. Because time must be allowed for settlement (the only reported transactions are those that have been paid for) and for reporting, the data end up being about two weeks old by the time they appear in the newspaper.

The psychology of short selling is interesting. Short selling of a particular stock tends to increase as the price of that stock drops, and the most frantic short selling is usually at the bottom of the security's price. For this reason, many short sellers can be hurt. If the stock price moves up, the investor may have to buy the shares back for his broker at a higher price than he received from the sale of the same shares. There is some pressure on the investor to buy the stock back under these conditions because the higher the price gets, the more money the short seller stands to lose. The difference between the two prices, the transaction costs, and the interest charged by the broker constitute the total loss to the investor.

When seeing a report of the monthly short selling on the exchanges, don't be misled by the absolute level of the figures (it's given as the number of shares). A highly active market can absorb a high level of short selling with no apparent effect. For a market at a low level of activity, the same amount of short selling could be newsworthy.

It is the ratio between the level of short selling and general market activity that is important. The short selling ratio provides just that: It is the total number of short interests on the exchange divided by the average daily trading volume for the reporting period. For the New York Stock Exchange there have been relatively few times that the ratio rose above 1.90.

Generally, one can take the short selling ratio as an indication of how convinced people are that the market is going down. On the other hand, some analysts feel that a high degree of short selling indicates market bottoms; most people are bearish and there are a lot of obligations (short sales) to eventually buy back stocks. Runups in some stock can be stimulated by short selling because if a stock is heavily shorted and begins moving up, many investors will run to cover—that is, purchase the stock to pay back to their brokers before it gets any higher. This buying pressure, of course, serves to drive the stock's price even higher.

There are other situations where short sales are used by arbitragers trying to profit when one company's stock is to be exchanged for another in a merger. If the price of the two different stocks, at whatever the ratio they are to be exchanged, is not exactly the same, then arbitragers can lock in the difference by buying the stock on one and sell the other short. They will have already purchased the stock to pay back at a lower price. The details of this technique are a bit complicated, but the important point is that the level of short selling can be artificially raised by arbitrage.

Short interest is followed closely and seems to be a useful indicator of market activity, particularly under one of the following conditions:

1. If the short selling ratio on the New York Stock Exchange reaches the 2.00 level, it is regarded as a bullish indication.

2. If the market in general has been declining for some time and suddenly short selling picks up, it may mean the market is overdue for a rise. With so many people jumping on the bandwagon (short selling) and the market already down, the stage is set for a rebound.

3. If short selling rises rapidly in a specific stock and then the stock itself begins reaching new highs, it is generally believed that the price rise is temporary. More short selling, however, can continue to propel the stock up.

SIXTEEN

Government Deficits and the Balance of Trade

The first example in this chapter gives an all-too-familiar picture of the month-to-month operations of the U.S. budget. Outlays are set off against receipts, and the result is a deficit. In our example, the report is for the fifth month of the government's fiscal year. A fiscal year means a *financial* year. For various reasons, the fiscal years of governments and businesses rarely coincide with calendar years. The U.S. government's fiscal year starts October 1 and ends on September 30.

Budgets are always designed for a specific period of time. Budgets for ongoing operations like governments or businesses are typically for one year. The monthly calculations of deficits or averages are simply interim reports. The results accumulate until the end of that year, at which time the government starts on a new fiscal year, and the deficit from the past year is added to the national debt. Since 1950 there have been only four years that the U.S. government has run a surplus. For every other year, the federal debt has grown.

LIVING WITH DEFICITS

One of the problems of maintaining a deficit is that it costs money. Debts must be financed by borrowings, and to borrow one must pay interest. As explained in the chapter on government securities, the government borrows by issuing bonds, notes, and bills. The interest that must be paid to investors who purchase these instruments is the cost, to the government, of these borrowings.

U.S. Budget Deficit Widens in February

WASHINGTON—The federal budget deficit is growing at an increased pace according to the U.S. Treasury. In February, the deficit stood at $20.83 billion, up from $20.38 billion a year earlier.

The Treasury, in its monthly budget statement, said that government receipts totaled $54.02 billion in February of the current fiscal year, and that federal outlays totaled $74.85 billion.

For the first five months of fiscal 1985 government receipts totaled $290.62 billion, and outlays totaled $390.27 billion. That produced a deficit of $99.64 billion.

Last month the government paid $12.95 billion just on the interest of the national debt.

When outlays exceed revenues, the result is a deficit. In the case of the federal government, monthly deficits are cumulative until the end of the fiscal year, at which time the deficit is added to the national debt.

The U.S. government is on a **fiscal year** that begins October 1.

Government deficits must be financed with borrowing. The U.S. government borrows through the issuance of government bonds, notes, and bills.

Interest on the national debt is, in fact, interest paid on government securities like bonds, notes, and bills.

The only way for a government to reduce its debt is to run a budget surplus, to take in more money than it spends. The surplus must then be used to pay off maturing debt (bonds, notes, etc.) rather than replacing them (rolling them over) with more debt.

The national debt is thus the sum of all the money the government has borrowed (and which is still outstanding) to finance budget deficits. Another way of looking at it is as the accumulation of all the past decisions of the government to borrow in order to pay debts rather than to raise taxes.

Deficit financing—that is, continuing to pay for government programs by increased amounts of debt—has become a way of life in the United States. It is hard to reverse this trend when many people strongly believe in what the government is spending the money for: defense, health care, highways, school lunches. It is obviously a matter of fiscal priorities. And government spending is not the only reason for a deficit budget. Economic slumps also contribute because revenues fall at the very same time that the need for unemployment benefits, food stamps, and other social programs increases.

Many observers and experts believe that a chronic deficit combined with a rising national debt is inflationary and adds a burden to future generations. On the other hand, some economists argue that the circumstances of the debt must be taken into consideration. For instance, government spending to get the country out of a prolonged economic depression can be worthwhile if it results in full employment and economic prosperity. Then incurred debt can be paid back relatively painlessly.

To many people, however, this is a no-win situation. The country either goes on paying huge amounts of interest year upon year, or it raises even larger amounts in taxes to pay off the principal. The ideal solution is increased prosperity, a period of full employment when the government runs a surplus and can assign the extra funds raised to reducing the national debt.

In considering methods by which the national debt can be reduced, it is interesting to take a closer look at where the interest that is generated by this debt goes. A large chunk of interest payments from government securities, about 20%, goes to other government agencies like the social security system. A bit less goes to the Federal Reserve banks which, by law, must return 90% of their profits to the Treasury. Another large chunk goes to U.S. bond, note, and bill holders. So in these three cases we are simply taking money out of one pocket and putting it into another. This, perhaps, makes the huge interest payments a bit less painful.

Real losses occur when payments are made to security holders outside the country. Because of prolonged high interest rates and the perception of the United States as a safe haven for investment, the proportion of foreign ownership of U.S. government securities has risen to about 25%. It has never been this high in the past, and the recent falling interest rates in this country may bring about a repatriation of foreign investments by investors outside the United States.

Another consideration that may help put the national debt in perspective is that it has grown at a slower pace than the economy in general, and even at its present 3% of the GNP, it is still lower than that of many leading industrial nations.

A vital and still unanswered question is whether deficit spending creates inflation. If so, then deficit spending cannot bring the prosperity necessary to provide a surplus budget which will, in turn, make it possible to lower the national debt. Businesses, saddled with high interest rates on their borrowings, simply cannot operate at full capacity.

One thing most economists do seem to agree on is that government borrowing during times of full employment and economic strength is counterproductive, since there will be no "better times" during which a budget surplus can be used to reduce the amounts borrowed. Clearly, to run a deficit budget in periods of economic prosperity is simply to put off the time when taxes must be raised to retire newly created debt.

THE U.S. BALANCE OF PAYMENTS

A balance of payments is a systematic record of a country's receipts from, or payments to, other countries. In a way, it is like the balance sheets we discussed for businesses, only on a national level.

As you can imagine, bookkeeping for an entire country is an enormous task, and it is made excruciatingly complex by the infinite variety of goods and services that flow between countries. The process is simplified somewhat because it is only the actual *payments* that enter and leave the country which are recorded, and not the movement of goods themselves (thus the term "balance of payments"). Each payment is categorized as to commodity, service, and so on and recorded as a debit if the funds leave the country and a credit if the funds enter the country.

There are three primary accounts in the balance of payments: the current account, the capital account, and the official settlement. They are shown below with their primary components. Any international payment or receipt is recorded in one of these categories.

In the worldwide flow of funds, it is interesting to note that the amount of money flowing through the capital account (investments and central bank transactions) is ten times larger than the amount flowing through the current account (goods and services, and foreign aid). This is partly because of the speed and ease with which massive amounts of money can be transferred across borders. The payment for 10,000 bushels of wheat, while it can be transferred with ease, still must wait until the physical commodity is transported before it is made.

BALANCE OF PAYMENT

I. Current Account
    A. Goods and services
        1. Merchandise trade ("visible" trade)
        2. Service ("invisible" trade)
    B. Foreign aid
II. Capital Account
    A. Private investments
    B. Transactions of central banks
III. Official Settlement

The references you see in the media to the "balance of trade" usually refer only to goods within the goods and services category of the current account. It is also known as merchandise or "visible" trade because it consists of tangibles like foodstuffs, manufactured goods, and raw materials. "Services," the other part of that category, is known as "invisible" trade and consists of intangibles such as interest or dividends, technology transfers, services (like insurance, transportation, financial), and so forth.

When the net result of both the current account and the capital account yields more credits than debits, the country is said to have a surplus in its balance of payments. When there are more debits than credits, the country has a deficit in the balance of payments. It is in the category of official settlement that any deficit is offset by official liabilities of the government or that surpluses are retained as U.S. official reserve assets. Deficits are usually offset by currency transfer transactions and obligations of official foreign bodies such as central banks.

SEVENTEEN

The Money Supply and the Federal Reserve

Money is essential to all but the most primitive economies. Money serves as a uniform standard of market value by defining those units with which we measure price. In the United States, that means dollars and cents. Money, however, is not only the measure of price; it also embodies value. That enables it to play its most important role of all: as a link between producers and consumers.

It is difficult to get a perspective on money without considering for a moment the economy in general. "Economy" has frequently been defined as the sum total of all the individual acts of production and consumption. But there is more to a country's economy than the collective acts of production and consumption; an economy is also made up of the way in which those separate acts interrelate.

WHY MONEY?

Individual goods and individual acts of production or service within a reasonably complex society can never be matched with (or set off by) other goods or acts of production or service. The values and varieties of all goods and services are simply too diverse. A standard medium of exchange, like money, is therefore essential. By means of money, any consumer can make a claim on any producer; so it is no distortion to regard the function of every dollar in the money supply as a potential claim on goods or services.

Obviously, an ingredient of the economy as important as the money supply is watched closely. When the money supply expands more rapidly than is required by the economy's production of goods and services, the additional money will cause prices to rise and stimulate inflation. On the other hand, if the growth of the money supply does not keep pace with the economy's production, prices will fall. If unchecked, production will slow, unemployment will rise, and, in the extreme, a depression will result.

Both inflation and depression have political as well as economic consequences. It is not surprising, therefore, that politicians have devised ways to control the money supply. In the past, some of these methods have proved successful and some have proved awkward, if not counterproductive.

Before discussing these measures, it is necessary to define money a bit more carefully. When we spoke of it earlier as a medium of exchange, we were able to limit ourselves to that which was generally accepted throughout the country in exchange for goods, services, or assets. Thus, for instance, items of barter are not considered money in the United States. But it is still necessary to break this definition down further. Money can be divided into two types:

1. *Currency:* This includes paper money and coins (and sometimes coins are not counted).

2. *Deposits:* These may be demand deposits, which include interest and non-interest-bearing checking accounts; and they may include deposits which are less accessible, such as savings accounts, money market funds, mutual funds, and instruments used primarily by institutional investors.

All money in the above categories is not of equal significance within the economy. Funds locked up in a nine-month certificate of deposit are less liquid than cash in one's pocket or the balance in one's checkbook. Liquidity or accessibility is the basis on which several categories of money have been developed for representing and measuring the money supply: M1, M2, and M3. M1, which stands for "Money One," is the narrowest and is made up of the most immediately accessible funds. It is primarily checkable accounts and cash in the hands of the public. The M2 category includes all of M1 and money which is not quite as liquid, such as savings accounts, time deposits, and money market and mutual funds. Those funds unique to M2 (not in M1) are thought to serve primarily as investment for their holders, rather than a medium of immediate exchange.

EXAMPLE 1. COMPONENTS OF THE M1 AND M2 MONEY SUPPLY

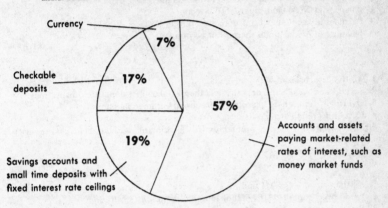

☐ = the M1 money supply

SOURCE: "What's All This About the M's?", Federal Reserve Bank of New York, July 1983.

It often comes as a surprise to people that currency, including cash and coins, constitutes such a small percentage of the money supply. Currency makes up only about 30% of M1 and a mere 7% of M2. The pie diagram in Example 1 illustrates the makeup of M1 and M2. The total of M1 (the shaded part of the pie) is only about a quarter of the total of M2.

It should be clear from Example 1 that most money in this country is not in the form of currency; it exists as numbers in bank accounts. This may seem a bit intangible for some people's tastes, but it is in keeping with the real world and how we use money. Most of us, for instance, pay bills with checks, and many incidentals are purchased with credit cards (soon to be followed by checks). Few of us carry enough cash for anything but trivial face-to-face transactions.

M3 is the broadest category of the money supply. It includes all of the previous two categories, as well as the major monetary instruments used by businesses. The precise makeup of each of the three categories is shown in the table below.

THE M CATEGORIES FOR MEASURING THE MONEY SUPPLY

M1

1. Currency (including coin) in the hands of the public
2. Travelers checks
3. Demand deposits (balances in checking accounts)
4. Balances in NOW and super-NOW accounts)
5. Balances in accounts with Automatic Transfer Service (ATS)
6. Balances in credit union share draft accounts

M2

1. All the categories of M1
2. Savings and small time deposits (less than $200,000) at depository institutions
3. Overnight repurchase agreements (repos) at commercial banks
4. Certain Eurodollar deposits
5. Shares in money market mutual funds held primarily by households and small businesses

M3

1. All the categories of M1 and M2
2. Large time deposits ($100,000 or more) at depository institutions
3. Repurchase agreements with maturities longer than one day at commercial banks and savings and loan associations
4. Shares in money market mutual funds which are used by large financial institutions and corporations

Source: "What's All This About the M's?", Federal Reserve Bank of New York, July 1983.

HOW MONEY IS CREATED

Money is created by loans. This may come as a surprise to those who thought the Treasury simply printed all the money it needed.

How easily the national debt could be paid if this were the case: Just print a few hundred billion-dollar Federal Reserve notes, and it would all be taken care of. Alas, it's not that easy. First of all, the Treasury doesn't print money; it only mints coins. All paper money is printed in Washington, D.C., by the Bureau of Engraving and Printing (it also prints stamps). Currency—that is, the physical printed bills—is distributed by the Federal Reserve banks, and they do so only to replace worn bills no longer fit for circulation. The average life expectancy of a dollar bill is about three months; other bills last somewhat longer. As unfit bills

Fed is short for Federal Reserve System. It is not a single bank, but is comprised of twelve Federal Reserve banks, one from each of the Federal Reserve regions.

Fed Monetary Policy Won't Be Tightened

WASHINGTON—The chairman of the Federal Reserve Board said yesterday that the nation's central bank decided not to tighten its monetary policy. The move was welcomed by Wall Street and could mean that interest rates will hold steady, instead of rising, for the next several months.

Investors responded positively to the news. Note and bond prices rose, and interest rates showed a sharp decline.

The stock market, in a recent slump, was also cheered. The Dow Jones industrial average gained 8.5 points yesterday to close at 1,018.43.

The chairman also announced that the Fed has tentatively decided to lower slightly its money supply growth target ranges for the year. . . .

The Federal Reserve Board is the governing body of the Federal Reserve System. It is made up of seven members appointed by the president of the United States (with confirmation by the Senate) for fourteen-year terms. The terms are staggered (two years apart), and one member is appointed chairman, by the president, for a four-year term.

Monetary policy refers to the management of the money supply. This has a direct effect on interest rates. (If money is scarce, interest rates go up.) This affects not only businesses, but individuals too in terms of interest rates on personal loans and credit cards.

If interest rates were to go up, both stock and bond markets would suffer. The market value of already-issued bonds would go down, since former interest rates would no longer be attractive. Dividends of stocks, too, would seem less appealing. Money would probably be drained from these instruments (depressing their prices further) and be placed in short-term money market instruments like CDs or money market funds.

come into the Federal Reserve banks they are weeded out and shredded, and new bills are put in their place.

Freshly printed money is introduced into the economy when unfit bills are replaced, and when bank customers demand more currency. As one would expect, Christmas is the time when the total amount of currency in circulation swells to its maximum for the year.

The myth that the government can simply print all the money it wants is so prevalent that it is worth considering for a moment just where the government gets money when it needs it. The primary source, of course, is taxes. But what does the government do when it needs the funds that it hasn't received in taxes yet? And, more serious, what does it do when its total obligations are more than its revenues? It does what the rest of us do: it borrows. That's what government bonds, notes, and bills are. The government borrows money on a massive scale, and in doing so it generates a huge body of government securities that figures heavily in the securities markets of this and many other nations.

But, returning to our original statement, how is money created through loans? Basically, it's like this. If you borrow a substantial amount of money from a bank, you don't go into the building with a wheelbarrow and carry the money out. Nor does the bank have a pile of money in its vaults of which it gives you a small amount. If you are granted a loan, it usually appears in the form of numbers in your checking account. Those numbers weren't there before. The bank simply creates the money by adding them to your account. You may take all or a part of it out, but that just means the numbers will wind up in someone else's bank account. Wherever they go, a large proportion of them will end up in bank accounts.

It should also be noted that this "created" money disappears as you pay back the loan. You may or may not take the money you are paying out of the same account, but you are taking it out of *some* account as you return it in monthly payments to the bank. The money, as it is paid back, disappears from the money supply.

Another fact about this "created" money is that it is not created out of nothing. It does have backing: it is backed by your obligation to pay what you owe.

At this point we have revealed an important clue about the money supply and how it can be controlled. When money is easy to borrow, the money supply increases; when it becomes difficult to borrow, the money supply shrinks. How do we make money difficult to borrow? By raising interest rates. Interest is literally the cost of borrowing money, and by raising the price, less money will be borrowed. Likewise, by lowering interest rates the cost of loans drops and the amount of money created through loans increases.

Obviously, there has to be some control on a bank's ability to create money through loans. The Federal Reserve regulates loans by requiring, among other things, that banks maintain reserves, either in vault cash or in deposits with their regional Federal Reserve bank, of a certain percent of their deposits. These reserves must be in cash, and they do not earn interest. The requirement that their federal reserves not earn interest is costly for banks, since interest is one of their major sources of revenues. Nevertheless, despite recent agitation for repeal, the requirement still stands.

Note that it is the deposits which are backed by reserves, not the loans. This is because the deposits are a liability of the bank (depositors could demand their money) and because a large percentage of created money is going to end up in bank accounts anyway. Whichever bank the created money is moved to will have to maintain the designated amount of reserves. This concept is called the "fractional reserve system."

An important aspect of the fractional reserve system is that money created by a loan can, in turn, generate even more money. For instance, with $3 million held in reserves, bank A can make approximately $20 million in loans, assuming a 15% reserve requirement. When removed from bank A, that amount may end up as deposits in banks B, C, and D, and collectively they must hold only $3 million in reserves and are free then to loan out the rest. The process may then be repeated over and over.

Every newly created amount of money, in turn, creates more than eight times its own value by the time it has been deposited and loaned out again for a (theoretically) indefinite number of times. This is obviously a powerful way to create money, and one which must not be abused. It is this process the Fed watches closely and over which it exercises partial control by means of the fractional reserve system.

THE FEDERAL RESERVE BANK

The Federal Reserve System in the United States is analogous to the central banks of other countries, such as the Bank of England or the Bank of Japan. The Federal Reserve System, is not, however, a single bank. It is a system made up of twelve Federal Reserve banks (one for each Federal Reserve region in the United

States) which are governed by a board of directors. When you see references to the "Fed" in the news, it is generally the board of the Federal Reserve System to which they refer; sometimes, it is the open market committee, the branch of the Fed that executes the market orders of the board (orders to buy or sell massive amounts of government securities on the open market).

The board of the Federal Reserve is appointed by the president of the United States with the approval of the Senate. The terms are for fourteen years and staggered so that one board member's term expires every two years. Such a long term of office guarantees that the board will be relatively free from political pressures. It is important to remember that the Fed is not an agency of the U.S. government; it is a corporation owned by its members, which are all federally chartered banks.

Founded in 1913, the Fed was originally intended to serve as the lender of last resort to help banks weather panics such as the one in 1907. A pool of money, created by member banks, would be used in these emergencies. Gradually, however, it became obvious that the Fed had the power to perform a much more important task—that of controlling the money supply. If the money supply could be controlled, perhaps the extremes of business cycles—inflation and depression—could be moderated.

By law, the Fed is now charged with this task. This means targeting rates of money growth within which it, the Fed, feels the nation's best interests are served. Further, it means taking appropriate action to bring the growth of the money supply to within these target ranges.

Congress has divided up money management of the nation's economy in the following way: Fiscal policy, which consists of raising taxes and appropriating funds, is reserved for itself. Monetary policy, which consists of regulating the money supply, it appropriated to the Fed.

HOW THE FED CONTROLS THE MONEY SUPPLY

The Fed's control over the money supply is far from comprehensive. Overall trends are hard to reverse, and there is a significant lag, sometimes of months, before economic indicators confirm the effectiveness of the Fed's actions or warn that the goals are not being met.

The Fed has three tools with which it can influence the money supply. The first is that it can change the amount of reserves commercial banks are required to hold against their deposits. In all our previous examples, it was assumed that the fractional reserve was 15%. It could be more or less, depending on the monetary policy of the Fed at the time.

If the Fed determines that there is not quite enough money in the country, it might lower the percentage amount the banks must hold in reserve. This means that more of the bank's money could be loaned out and that interest rates will probably be lowered slightly. If the Fed wished to restrict the growth of the money supply, it could raise the percentage requirement of reserves. This will make money more scarce and raise interest rates.

A change in the reserve requirement is not a subtle tool. Even a small change abruptly affects massive amounts of money, and the effect can sometimes be hard to control. This tool is therefore used infrequently, and then only when strong and decisive action is required.

The second tool of the Fed, open market operations, can be thought of as the fine-tuning device for implementing monetary policy. In the Federal Reserve Bank of New York, a trading office is maintained for buying and selling government securities. If the Fed decides to restrict monetary growth, it can take money out of the system by selling massive amounts of U.S. securities. When a bank purchases U.S. securities, the cash moving into the Fed goes out of circulation and is no longer a part of the money supply. The bank has securities which it cannot use as its federally required reserves. (Remember, such reserves must be in special reserve accounts or vault cash and does not draw interest.) Therefore, the Fed, by selling securities, has removed cash from the money supply and limited the banks' ability to generate new money through loans.

By the same token, when the Fed wishes to encourage the growth of the money supply, it buys securities. (It always buys or sells only its own instruments, U.S. bonds, notes, or bills.) The cash it puts out for these securities can serve as Fed reserves and therefore automatically constitutes reserves which the bank can use to create new money. While this tactic usually works, it is not foolproof or immediate. Sometimes banks hold additional money in their reserves (known as "excess reserves") and refuse to create new loans. Some money may also be absorbed into time deposits, which are not counted as part of the M1.

While the policies are decided by the board of the Federal Reserve, the specifics are worked out by the open market committee. The Fed will pay whatever the market demands in order to obtain the securities it wants and will receive whatever price it must (albeit the highest of the prices offered) when it sells securities. The Fed thus becomes another player in the free market system. The government does not legislate prices, but its activity does affect prices, just like any other major purchaser of securities does.

The third tool of the Fed for controlling the money supply is the rates it charges banks for borrowing at the discount window. The overall process is a bit complex, but it goes something like this. The banks, as mentioned before, must keep a certain percentage of their deposits in reserve. These reserves must maintain the required percentage every day. Since total deposits at any bank will vary daily, there is some cushion maintained to absorb the expected everyday fluctuations. Frequently, however, a bank will find that its reserves are short. This can happen particularly in a period of heavy borrowing, since the borrowed funds are likely to end up in account balances.

Whenever the bank finds its reserves short, it must borrow the necessary funds from its regional Federal Reserve bank. This is called borrowing at the discount window. The rates are generally low, and it is expected that banks will not need to avail themselves of this service frequently. Nevertheless, millions are available, generally only for overnight, through the discount window. When the Fed is restricting monetary growth, the discount rate rises, making banks increasingly reluctant to borrow in this manner. In a period of looser monetary policy, the discount rate will drop. This cost of money for the banks will be passed along to their customers in the form of higher (or lower) interest rates.

GLOSSARY

Terms and Jargon of the Financial News

accrued interest   The amount of interest accumulated since the last interest payment. In the case of most bonds, accrued interest must be added to the purchase price. Note that that amount will be recovered by the investor, since the following interest payment will be for the entire interest period.

acid test ratio   The quick assets (current assets minus inventory) divided by the current liabilities. This is similar to the current ratio, except that the current ratio uses the current assets, a balance sheet item, divided by the current liabilities.

actuals   The physical commodities as distinguished from futures contracts. Actuals, also called cash commodities or spot commodities, are on hand and ready for delivery or storage. They are sold on, and their prices are quoted on, cash markets; also called spot markets.

adjustment bond   *See* income bond.

ADR   *See* American depository receipt.

aftermarket   Trading in a new issue, either OTC or on an exchange, immediately following the initial distribution.

agency bond   *See* authority bond.

American depository receipts (ADR)   Certificates issued by a U.S. bank and traded in this country the same way that domestic shares are. They represent a specific number of foreign securities held by a U.S. banking institution in the country of origin. This practice facilitates the trading of foreign securities within the United States by eliminating currency exchange, legal obstacles, foreign ownership transfers, the necessity of trading on a foreign exchange, and the problems of bearer form stock certificates, which are not used in this country.

American Stock Exchange (ASE or AMEX)   The second largest stock exchange in the United States. It also handles transactions in bonds and options. At one time it was called the "curb" exchange because it originated as an outdoor market near Wall Street.

AMEX *See* American Stock Exchange.

amortization A provision for the gradual reduction of an obligation or the gradual decline in value of an asset. For depreciation, it is the spreading out of the entire depreciation amount over a period of years.

annual report A comprehensive financial statement issued yearly by corporations. The reports are highly regulated and should present a clear picture of the financial condition of a company. Also included are announcements of new products or services, explanations of past performance, and statements of future prospects. Copies are sent to shareholders and are available to other interested parties on request.

annualized percent Statement of the percent yield from a debt instrument maturing in less than a year stated as if the yield of the instrument would continue at the same rate for the remainder of the year. It is understood that the amount yielded so far from that instrument will be in the same proportion to its annual yield that the instrument's time to maturity is to one year.

arbitrage (pronounced ar'bitrazh') The simultaneous purchase on one exchange and sale on another of the same or equivalent financial instruments (such as stocks, option, futures) or commodities in order to profit from any price differences between them. Often the differences are so slight that such transactions are profitable only to exchange traders who do not pay retail commissions. *See* risk arbitrage.

as agent The usual role of a brokerage when it undertakes securities transactions for clients. Broker commissions are charged for this service. *See* as principal.

ASE *See* American Stock Exchange.

ask or **asked price** *See* bid and asked prices.

as principal When a brokerage buys or sells securities for or from its own account. In the case of a sale to a client, the asked price is charged without commission. This is also called "making a market" in a security.

assets Everything owned by a corporation and that is due it. Fixed assets include buildings and machinery; current assets include inventory and accounts receivable; intangible assets include patents and even goodwill.

assign The designation of an option writer for the fulfillment of the terms of an option that the investor previously sold. The Options Clearing Corporation (OCC) randomly makes the assignment to brokerages which in turn (and by a variety of methods) must decide to which client the assignment will be given. *See* exercise.

at-the-market   Also called a "market order." An order to buy or sell immediately at the best price available. This is the most common mode of securities transaction.

authority bond   Municipal bond issued by a local political authority undertaking a public project such as a hospital or a toll road. The same as an agency bond.

authorized stock   The maximum amount of stock stipulated in the certificate of incorporation that a corporation may issue. This includes unissued stock and issued stock. A company is represented only by issued stock. The latter is made up of stock issued and outstanding (in the hands of the public), and treasury stock *(q.v.)*.

automatic exercise   A procedure whereby an in-the-money option is automatically exercised just before expiration by the brokerage or the OCC on behalf of the holder.

average down   The purchase of additional shares of the same security after a drop in prices so that the average of the two (or more) purchase prices will be lower than the initial market price that was paid.

baby bond   A bond with less than $1,000 par value, usually $100.

balance sheet   Section of an annual report that gives the financial picture of a corporation as of the last day of the fiscal year or quarter. Dollar value of assets is weighed against the liabilities and owners' equity. A "consolidated" balance sheet includes figures for all subsidiaries.

balloon effect   Successively increased principal repayments.

BAN   *See* bond anticipation note.

bankers' acceptances   Negotiable short-term instruments issued by U.S. banks with which U.S. companies pay foreign trade debts. Foreign banks may redeem these certificates at the issuing U.S. bank or sell them to a third party. Their yields are close to those of large certificates of deposit.

basis grade   A commodity grade specified by an exchange as acceptable for delivery on a futures contract.

basis point   One percent of 1 percent. Often used in comparing yields of fixed-income securities. 10.15 percent and 10.16 percent differ by 1 basis point.

bear   An investor who expects prices on securities markets to decline, particularly one who invests so as to profit by such a decline.

bear market   A market in which the prices are declining or one in which the prices are already low.

bearer bond   *See* bearer form.

bearer form   A form in which bonds are issued, also called coupon form, in which coupons are attached to the bond certificate. No record is kept by the issuing company, so that the bearer (presumed owner) must clip the coupons and return them to the company or its agent in order to receive interest payments. No bonds in the United States are currently issued in this manner, although many older municipal bonds are still in this form.

beta   An indication of the relationship of the price movement of a specified security to the movement of the market as a whole. A stock with a low beta is expected to be more stable in its price movements than the market in general.

bid and **asked prices**   A bid price is a price at which a broker has offered to purchase a security or commodity; it is the price you will receive should you sell. The asked price is the price at which a broker has offered to sell a security or commodity; it is the price you will pay should you purchase. Some NASDAQ stock quotations list both prices for OTC stock, although the tendency now is to list transaction prices, as is done for exchange-listed securities. In the NASDAQ system the bid and asked prices are firm offers from brokers who are making a market in that particular security. The difference between the two prices is called the spread and constitutes the profit for the market maker in transactions of this stock. The more actively the stock is traded, the smaller the spread. Bid and asked prices are part of all exchange trading, but only the transaction price is usually reported.

big board   The New York Stock Exchange.

block   A large number of shares, usually over 10,000.

blue chip   Common stock that is thought to be of the highest quality. These are usually higher-priced shares of stable, long-established companies that have paid dividends regularly.

blue-sky law   State laws concerning registration and sale of new securities. Intended to protect the public against fraud, the term refers to the alleged statement of a judge to the effect that a particular stock had about the same value as a patch of blue sky.

bond   A long-term debt instrument (the issuer is the borrower) usually with a fixed interest rate (coupon rate) and a maturity date at which the face value (par value) will be returned to the purchaser. Bonds may be divided into four broad classifications, depending on the issuer: corporate bonds, municipal bonds, government bonds, and government agency bonds. When compared to other debt instruments, bonds are the longest term; notes are generally shorter, and bills are the shortest.

book value   The net worth or net assets of a corporation (assets minus liabilities) divided by the number of common shares outstanding after deducting the liquidation price of all preferred stock; an attempt to give a tangible value to the shares of a company. This is, presumably, the return to the shareholder if the company were liquidated; sometimes called equity capital or stockholders' equity.

breakout In technical analysis, a term for the rise or fall of the market price of a security through a level where it had been stopped before.

broker A licensed agent who executes public orders in securities or commodities for a commission. The term is often applied to, but does not necessarily include, registered representatives within a brokerage.

brokerage A firm that executes public orders for securities or commodities. Also, the commission received by a broker.

brokers' loans Money borrowed from banks by brokers in order to buy securities, finance new issues, or carry their clients' margin accounts. The interest rates charged by banks for these loans are watched closely by the securities industry.

bucket shop Various illegal practices with regard to customers' orders, such as accepting them but not executing them in an attempt to obtain lower prices while charging the client the original prices.

bull An investor who expects prices on markets to rise, particularly one who invests so as to profit by such a rise.

bull market A market on which the prices are rising or on which the prices are, on the average, already high.

bull spread An option strategy that can be implemented by a combination of either puts or calls in which certain risks are eliminated and a profit can be made if there is a rise in the price of the underlying security.

butterfly spread An option strategy constructed of either puts or calls that involves both a bull spread and a bear spread. There are three striking prices, with the middle one shared by both spreads.

calendar spread A combination of two options of the same type (puts or calls) both with the same strike price, but different expiration dates.

call An option giving the right to purchase 100 shares of a specific stock, at a specific price, within a specific time period.

callable A bond or preferred stock which has a call feature *(q.v.)*.

call feature (1) A stipulation of a bond issue whereby the issuer may redeem the bonds before maturity for a specified price (the call price) and under specified conditions. (2) A similar stipulation for a preferred stock issue whereby the stock may be bought back by the issuer at a price equal to or slightly higher than either the par value or the market price.

call protection   A feature of some bonds and preferred stock whereby they cannot be called or at least cannot be called before a specified date.

capital   Money used to start or to expand a business. Also refers to capital goods, which consist of equipment, machinery, tools, and so on used in production.

capital gain or **capital loss**   The profit or loss from the sale of securities over (or under) the original purchase price. Does not include interest. If a bond is sold at a higher price than that for which it was paid, the difference is capital gain. The interest received in the meantime is not. Interest from discounted debt instruments is not capital gains. Capital gains from securities held longer than one year are taxed at a lower rate than those held less than one year.

cash commodity   *See* actuals.

cash flow   Net income minus noncash revenues (if any) plus depreciation and any other items charged to reserves that were not actually paid out in dollars.

cash forward sale   The sale of a commodity (as opposed to a future) for delivery at a later date.

cash market   The purchase or sale of actuals or cash commodities (as opposed to futures); also called spot market. Sometimes the term is used only for grains, and spot market is used for the actuals of other commodities.

CBOE   Chicago Board of Options Exchange.

CBT   Chicago Board of Trade.

certificate of deposit (CD)   The negotiable certificate of deposit is a receipt for funds that have been deposited in a bank for a specified period of time and at a fixed rate of interest. Certificates for $100,000 or more may be traded on the secondary market. Their maturities range from one to eighteen months, although the ninety-day CD is standard. Most are issued with an interest-bearing coupon, although some are issued at a discount.

CFTC   Commodity Futures Trading Commission.

changes in stockholders' equity   (also known as statement of stockholders' equity) A section of the annual report showing the stockholders' equity—the difference between assets and liabilities.

churning   Frequent buying and selling of securities with little purpose other than to generate commissions for the broker.

class   In options, it distinguishes puts from calls. Options of the same class would be only puts or only calls. In stocks, classes are used to distinguish between issues of preferred or of common stocks that have some significant difference (such as different dividend rates, or a different number of votes in corporate elections).

close corporation *See* closely held.

closed-end investment company A company formed for the purpose of investing in other securities. It is "closed end" in that there are a set number of shares (as with all corporations), which distinguishes it from a mutual fund.

closely held A corporation owned by a few stockholders. Legally, it is a corporation on which the law imposes restrictions not only on the number of shareholders, but on the transferability of the shares too. Ordinary investors cannot usually purchase them. Also, instead of a board of directors, there is a body called the "management."

closing price The last transaction price for a security during a trading day.

closing transaction An options or a futures transaction (purchase or sale) that cancels a previous position. Except for the premium, it must have the same terms as the option it closes. For example, if one has sold a put, one closes by buying a put with the same terms.

CME Chicago Mercantile Exchange.

coincident economic indicators Economic indicators which track the present state of an industry sector or the economy. *See* Index of Coincident Economic Indicators.

collateral trust bond A mortgage or debenture bond issue that is at least in part secured by a stock or bond portfolio.

combination A combination option position other than a straddle which is made up of both puts and calls.

COMEX Commodity Exchange, Inc., of New York.

commercial paper Short-term unsecured debt obligations issued by corporations. Sold at discount in denominations of $100,000 and over.

commission A broker's fee for handling securities or commodity transactions.

commodity A farm product such as grain or cotton; a mineral such as gold or copper; a forest product such as lumber or plywood. Sometimes the term is used for financial instruments such as CDs or Treasury bills. Commodities traded on an exchange must have sufficient supply and demand and be divisible into standard units, and some must be gradable with respect to quality.

commodity future *See* futures contract. Sometimes this term is used to distinguish farm product or mineral futures from financial futures.

common stock   A unit of ownership in a corporation. Distinguished from preferred stock because the latter has, among other differences, a set dividend rate.

common stock equivalents   Any securities, such as bonds and preferred stock, that can be converted into common stock of the same company.

competitive bid   Literally, a bid that is competing with other bids. In the purchase of government securities, it refers to the bids submitted from brokerage houses that specialize in government securities (or sometimes other parties) to a Treasury auction for new government issues. Bids from individuals are always noncompetitive *(q.v.)*.

consolidated balance sheet   *See* balance sheet.

consolidated tape   A system that continuously reports every transaction on all exchanges linked by the Intermarket Trading System—that is, both national exchanges and five regional exchanges. Network A reports on all NYSE-listed stocks, and network B reports on all AMEX-listed stocks. This is commonly known as the ticker tape. Reports are flashed to ticker displays on all exchanges. After a 15-minute delay, they are broadcast to all other ticker machines, displays, and on cable television.

consumer price index   This index measures the price of a fixed "basket" of 385 goods and services that are selected because of their direct effect on the majority of consumers in the country. Included are such things as food, housing, medical care, and fuel. It is considered the major measure of inflation. There are two indexes, the Consumer Price Index for All Urban Consumers (C.P.I.-U) and the Consumer Price Index for Urban Wage Earners and Clerical Workers (C.P.I.-W). The former is the one usually reported in the news.

conversion   *See* convertible.

conversion parity   A state whereby the market price of a convertible bond (or convertible preferred stock) and the securities into which they can be converted equal the same amount of dollars.

conversion price   The resultant value of the underlying security when converted into the common stock at the conversion ratio. If the conversion ratio is 50 (50 shares per $1,000 bond), then the conversion price of the underlying stock is $20.

conversion ratio   The number of shares (usually common stock) of the same company into which a convertible security (bond or preferred stock) may be converted. The conversion ratio is adjusted for stock splits.

convertible A feature of some bonds, preferred stocks, and shares of mutual funds. For a bond or preferred stock, it permits conversion into a stated amount of common stock of the same company under specified conditions. For mutual funds, it permits the holder of shares in one fund to exchange them for shares of comparable value in another fund managed by the same company.

cornering the market Control of enough securities, options, or commodity futures to permit price manipulation. In commodities it can mean, in extreme cases, acquisition of more futures contracts than existing supplies of the commodity can meet.

corporate bond A long-term debt instrument issued by a corporation (including railroads and public utilities); one of the major categories of bonds.

corporation A form of business organization chartered by, and to an extent regulated by, a state. The shares of closed or privately held corporations *(q.v.)* are usually owned by relatively few individuals. The shares of public companies are owned by many persons and traded OTC or on one or more exchanges. The liability of the owners (the shareholders) for the debts of the corporation is only to the extent of their investment.

coupon bond *See* bearer form.

coupon rate The fixed rate of interest paid by a bond.

cover A closing transaction for an option that was previously sold.

covered option An option that is sold when the writer (seller) owns the underlying security or is in possession of another option with the same terms.

covering *See* short covering.

cumulative preferred stock An issue of preferred stock on which back dividends accumulate should any be omitted. The payment of cumulative dividends takes priority over the dividends of common stock.

curb exchange old name for the American Stock Exchange because trading of securities was initially done in the street.

current assets Cash and all assets likely to be converted to cash within the fiscal year, such as accounts receivable.

current liabilities Debts of a company payable within the fiscal year.

current ratio Current assets divided by the current liabilities. This is also known as the working capital ratio.

current yield The percent of the purchase price of a stock or a bond returned by the annual dividend or interest payments.

CUSIP number An identification number appearing on the face of security documents and certificates which stands for Committee of Uniform Security Identification Procedure. On recent stock certificates, it usually appear in the right-hand area, preceded by the letters CUSIP. Each security is assigned its own identification number.

customer's man Former term for registered representative.

CV Abbreviation often used in stock and bond quotations to indicate that the security is convertible *(q.v.)*.

date of record Last day before a stock goes ex-dividend. Shareholders registered in corporate books on that day have been registered in time to receive the current dividend.

dealer A securities firm that buys or sells specific securities as principal *(q.v.)*.

debenture A commonly issued unsecured bond backed by the full faith and credit of the issuer but not by tangible assets.

debt instrument Usually used to refer to bonds; in the case of the government, bonds, notes, and bills.

debt to equity ratio Ratio of a company's long-term debt to the shareholder's equity.

default Failure of the issuer of a bond to pay interest due or principal at maturity or to pay interest due on preferred stock. In commodities it is the failure to make or take delivery as required by a futures contract.

delivery The fulfillment of an option exercise or a futures contract by tendering stock (in the case of options) or a commodity (in the case of futures).

delivery date Day specified on futures contract for delivery. It is always preceded by a delivery notice assigned by the clearing house.

delivery notice Notice from the seller of intent to deliver on a particular date. The notices are assigned to the buyer by the clearing house, and they specify grade and place of delivery.

depreciation An amount charged against earnings, representing the decline in value of assets. Often, depreciation is deducted from the fixed assets before they are listed in the balance sheet. Ideally, depreciation will be amortized over the useful life of an asset. The government makes tax allowances for depreciation; there is no cash outlay on the part of the company. Allowances for depreciation over the year can assist in the replacement of the asset being depreciated.

designated order turnaround (DOT) A computerized system that automatically routes small security orders to the appropriate stock specialist.

diagonal spread The simultaneous purchase and sale of calls and puts on the same security with different strike prices and different expiration dates.

diluted earnings per share *See* earnings per share.

discount (1) The amount bonds and preferred stock are selling below their face value. (2) The pricing of an option below its intrinsic value. (3) Also means "to take into account" in the sense that a current stock price which has dropped could be said to have discounted the news of an expected cut in dividends.

discount rate The rate of interest charged by a Federal Reserve bank for member banks to borrow their federally required reserves.

diversification The spreading of investments among different companies in different industries, sometimes in different countries, and sometimes among different investment media, such as precious metals, in order to reduce risk.

dividend An amount declared by the board of directors of a corporation to be paid per share to the shareholders. Usually in cash, it is sometimes paid in stock. The amount can vary according to the fortunes of the company, and sometimes it can be paid from past earnings if current earnings are insufficient. For preferred shares, the amount is fixed and does not change under ordinary circumstances.

dollar cost averaging A long-term system of buying securities at regular intervals and at fixed dollar amounts no matter what the current price fluctuations. The resulting total price for the investor will be the average of all prices paid.

DOT *See* designated order turnaround.

double taxation government taxation of dividends to shareholders after the corporation has already paid tax on the profit out of which the dividends are drawn.

Dow Jones averages Market averages from three industry groups: the industrial average is taken from 30 industrial stocks; the transportation average is taken from 20 transportation stocks; and the utilities average is taken from 15 public utilities stocks. The average within each area is determined by dividing the closing prices of each security by a divisor that compensates for past stock splits. The composite average includes all the above stocks. This is the oldest and most widely used stock market average. It is what is called a "narrow" indicator, since it is calculated from so few issues.

downside protection Indicates a range through which the security price could fall before there is a loss. Can also refer to protection against a fall in price.

down tick A transaction at a price less than the previous one. Also called a *minus tick*.

dually listed   A security that trades on more than one exchange.

dual purpose company   A closed-end investment company that initially issues two classes of stock: income shares and capital shares.

earnings   The total net profit of a company per year. In annual reports it is also given as a per share figure in the income statement. Earnings are vital in the fundamental evaluation of a stock. Brief earnings reports are often grouped together in the financial pages of newspapers; they give earnings for the current year (or quarter) and compare them to the earnings for the previous year (or quarter). Primary earnings per share is the earnings per share for the number of shares outstanding as of the beginning of the report period. Diluted earnings per share is the same except that it assumes all instruments with conversion capability (into common shares) have been converted.

earnings per share   *See* earnings.

earnings report   *see* income statement.

economic indicator   A statistical series or an index that represents the changes in an industry or economic sector. There are three recognized indicators in the United States: leading indicators, coincident indicators, and lagging indicators *(q.v.)*.

equipment trust bond   A bond for which machinery or equipment (such as railroad cars) is used as collateral.

equity   Commonly used to refer to ownership interest in a company by means of common or preferred stock. It is also used to refer to the excess value of property or stock in a company over and above any indebtedness. When applied to a margin account, it refers to the total value of the securities above the debit balance.

equity instrument   stock.

equivalent taxable yield   The percentage yield you would have to receive from a corporate bond in order to keep the same amount of money you would keep from a tax-free bond.

ex-distribution   The day after a distribution, such as a stock dividend, to which a new purchaser will not be entitled.

ex-dividend   The day after a dividend has been paid and to which a new purchaser will not be entitled.

exercise   Notification by the holder of an option that he or she requests fulfillment of the terms of the option contract.

exercise limit   A limit on the number of options one holder may exercise within a stated period of time. Set by exchanges to prevent cornering of the market.

exercise notice   The document sent to the Options Clearing Corporation by an option holder requiring fulfillment of the terms of the option by the individual to whom it is assigned.

exercise price   The price stipulated by the option contract at which the holder can buy or sell the underlying security. Also called a *strike price*.

ex-rights   Securities which formerly traded in units that contained rights but which are now trading without them because they have been removed or have expired.

extra   Often used to mean an extra dividend.

extraordinary item   An item of either income or expense that is not expected to recur.

ex-warrants   Securities which formerly traded in units that contained warrants but which are now trading without them because they have been removed or they have expired.

face value   The price at which a bond is redeemed at maturity and on which the coupon rate is calculated. Also called par value.

FDIC   *See* Federal Deposit Insurance Corporation.

Federal Deposit Insurance Corporation   A federal agency that provides insurance for bank deposits.

Federal Home Loan Bank (FHLB)   A government-sponsored agency that issues bonds for the purpose of making mortgages available to the home building industry. Interest is exempt from state and local income taxes.

Federal Intermediate Credit Bank (FICB)   A government-sponsored agency that issues bonds for the purpose of making loans available to farming and production interests. Interest is exempt from state and local income tax.

Federal Land Bank (FLB)   A government-sponsored corporation that issues bonds for the purpose of making mortgages available to farms and agricultural concerns. Interest is exempt from state and local income tax.

Federal National Mortgage Association (FNMA)   Known as Fannie Mae, this government-sponsored corporation (publicly owned) engages in the purchase and sale of FHA, FHDA, or VA mortgages. Interest is exempt from state and local income tax.

Fed   *See* Federal Reserve System.

Federal Reserve bank   One of the twelve banks that form the Federal Reserve System. There is one in each of the twelve Federal Reserve districts into which the United States is divided.

Federal Reserve Board   *See* Federal Reserve System.

Federal Reserve System   The central bank of the United States. Among its jobs is regulation of the money supply (monetary policy) and regulation of credit. It consists of twelve regional banks and is governed by a board of directors. References to the Fed are usually to the board of the Federal Reserve System.

fiduciary   An institution or an individual to whom property is entrusted for the benefit of another.

first in, first out (FIFO)   A manner of listing the value of the inventory on the balance sheet using the cost of the oldest items in the inventory, as opposed to the LIFO system *(q.v.)*.

first notice day   The first day that notices of intention to deliver can be sent to sellers (those in short positions) through the various commodity clearinghouses.

fiscal policy   Management of taxes and public expenditures. This is the role Congress has reserved for itself. It is distinct from monetary policy *(q.v.)*, which is delegated to the Federal Reserve System.

fiscal year   The bookkeeping year for a corporation. It may begin (and end) at any time during the calendar year.

fixed asset   Any asset that is utilized in current operations and expected to be used for more than a year, such as factories or machinery.

fixed liabilities   debt obligations that mature in over a year or are expected to last longer than a year.

flat   The condition under which a bond is traded without accrued interest.

floating-rate notes   Bonds whose interest rates are tied to and periodically adjusted to (a percent of) the rates of some other financial instrument, such as Treasury bills.

floor broker   A trader on the floor of an exchange who physically executes orders.

flower bond   A Treasury bond that may be redeemed at par value upon the death of the owner for the purpose of application to inheritance tax.

fourth market   Direct securities transactions between large institutions without the services of a broker.

fully diluted earnings per share   An earnings figure that represents the maximum possible dilution—that is, an earnings figure calculated as if all convertible securities had been exchanged for common stock.

fully registered bond   A bond whose holders are registered on the books of the issuing company. Interest payments and redemption of par at maturity are automatically mailed.

fundamental analysis   The study of a company and its securities that employs aspects of accounting, that examines management, and that views the company in the broader context of market conditions.

fungible   The interchangeability of one thing for another. This is a characteristic of most investment instruments; for example, one share of a company is interchangeable with any other share of the same company.

futures contract   An agreement to deliver a stated quality and quantity of a commodity, currency, or financial instrument. If one buys a futures contract (goes "long"), one is in the position of eventually receiving the commodity and paying the stated price unless the position is liquidated. If one sells a futures contract (goes "short"), one is in the position of eventually delivering the commodity and accepting the stated price.

general obligation bond   A municipal bond backed by the full faith and credit of the issuer.

GNP   *See* gross national product.

golden parachute   Lucrative bailout measures for executives such as severance pay or stock allowances that come into effect in the case of a takeover.

Government National Mortgage Association (GNMA)   Called Ginnie Mae, a government corporation that buys mortgages backed by the FHA and VA. Bonds are issued on pools of mortgages. Payments of principal and interest from the mortgages are passed through the corporation to the investor monthly.

Gross national product (GNP)   Total of all goods and services produced in the United States valued at current market prices in current dollars. Real GNP represents the same figure adjusted for inflation.

growth stock   Stock with prospects for rapid appreciation in value. Not necessarily smaller or younger companies, these are companies with, for example, increased market potential or new technologies.

guaranteed bonds   Bonds guaranteed by a company other than the issuer.

hedge   The holding of the combination of a long position and a short position in the same security, option, commodity, or future where a loss in one position is offset by a gain in the other. The strategy is not so much for gains as to avoid loss. Such a position can be used to prevent the decline in value of a fixed-income portfolio or to guarantee the price of a commodity to be needed in the future. In commodities, a hedger is also one who deals in the physical commodity but who makes use of the price differences between the cash market and futures market for protection and for profit.

holder One who holds a security.

holder of record The individual (or institution) who owns the security on the record date—that is, the legal day on which dividends are distributed (the day before the security goes ex-dividend).

holding company An investment company with holdings (often majority holdings) in other companies.

horizontal spread A calendar spread *(q.v.)*.

hot issue A new issue, available from investment bankers, whose price is expected to rise immediately upon initial trading in the after-market (as soon as it becomes available OTC or on an exchange).

IMM *See* International Monetary Market.

in the money An option with intrinsic worth—either a call with a striking price below the current market price of the underlying security, or a put with a striking price above the current market price of the underlying security.

income bond A bond whose interest is paid only if earnings permit; sometimes issued by companies in financial difficulty. For some issues, the interest is partially cumulative. The principal is under obligation to be paid at maturity.

income shares One of a type of shares issued by dual-purpose funds with guaranteed minimum dividends. The other type is capital gains shares.

income statement Also known as a statement of operation or profit and loss statement, this is a section of a corporation's annual report giving the cumulative earnings and profitability as a result of the former year's operations. Total income is given, as well as the cost of sales. Here you will see whether the company made or lost money. Also gives per share earnings.

indenture The terms of a debt instrument such as a bond.

index A relative measure of changes in prices, sales, production, etc., calculated from an arbitrary value assigned to a specific year (or years).

Index of Coincident Economic Indicators An index made up of a collection of indicators published by the U.S. Department of Commerce that are believed to reliably represent the present state of the economy. It contains indicators such as personal income and retail sales and is expected to confirm the earlier findings of the Index of Leading Economic Indicators.

Index of Lagging Economic Indicators An index made up of a collection of indicators published by the U.S. Department of Commerce that are believed to confirm, after the fact, the condition of the economy. It consists of indicators such as business loans outstanding and the book value of trade inventories. This index is looked to to confirm the earlier findings of the Index of Leading Economic Indicators and the Index of Coincident Economic Indicators.

Index of Leading Economic Indicators An index made from a collection of indicators published by the U.S. Department of Commerce that are believed to predict future trends in the economy. Some of the indicators included are unemployment, factory orders, and the money supply.

individual proprietorship Ownership of a business by a single individual. The simplest and most common form in which business is conducted in the United States.

industrial revenue bond A type of municipal bond issued to raise funds for the construction of facilities for corporations. Proceeds from the facility pay the interest and principal of the bond.

inflation A rise in prices throughout the economy generally indicative of a lessening of the value of the currency.

initial distribution *See* primary distribution.

insider A member of the board, an officer, or even a stockholder who is privy to nonpublic information about a company, particularly of a kind that would affect the price of that company's securities. Also includes members of that person's immediate family.

institutional investor A large organization or a branch of a large organization whose primary function is to invest its assets or assets entrusted to it. Includes mutual funds, pension funds, insurance companies, banks, and many others.

instrument Synonymous with "security." Sometimes implies a shorter-term vehicle than the latter.

intangible asset An item which is regarded as having value by the company even though it does not have tangible existence, such as goodwill, reputation, and patents.

interest The amount a lender gives a borrower (in addition to the return of the principal) in payment for the use of the principal.

International Bank for Reconstruction and Development A bank set up to make industrial loans to various countries who are members. The United States controls 25 percent interest.

International Monetary Market (IMM) A division of the Chicago

Mercantile Exchange on which futures are traded for Treasury bills, gold, silver, copper, and foreign currencies.

intrinsic value   The amount that an option is in the money *(q.v.)*.

inventory   An item on the balance sheet which includes the value of raw materials as well as manufactured goods in every stage of processing.

investment   The use of money in such a way as to yield more money while at the same time protecting capital and minimizing the risk to less than that of gambling.

investment banker   An individual or institution that underwrites new securities. An investment banker buys the securities from the company, thus guaranteeing the company the capital it seeks, and in turn sells the securities, at a markup, to the public or institutions.

investment club   A group of people usually formed into a partnership who pool their resources to invest and to socialize. They are member-managed and not usually constituted of professional investors.

investment company   A company that invests in other companies. Investment companies have the advantages of pooled resources and professional management. There are closed-end investment companies and open-end investment companies; the latter are mutual funds.

investment value   Applied to a convertible security, it is the estimated market price of a security if it had no conversion feature. In other words, the price at which the security would have to sell to bring its yield into line with the yield percent available from comparable nonconvertible securities.

issue   Any of the various types of securities of a company that are at least partially in the hands of the public.

issued and outstanding   Stock in the hands of the public or the directors of the corporation.

issued stock   The amount of stock issued and outstanding (in public hands) and the amount held by the corporation as treasury stock *(q.v.)*. Note that this total number may be less than the amount of stock the certificate of incorporation permits, and that the board may decide to issue additional shares up to that amount. *See* authorized stock.

job lot   In commodity futures (and sometimes other types of transactions), a unit of trading less than a round lot.

lagging economic indicators   Economic indicators that are expected to confirm, after the fact, the condition of an industry sector or the economy.

last in/first out (LIFO) A manner of listing the inventory on the balance sheet. Uses production cost of the most recent items in the inventory, as opposed to the FIFO *(q.v.)* system.

leading economic indicators economic indicators such as the unemployment rate or factory orders which predict the future state of an industry sector or the economy. *See* Index of Leading Economic Indicators.

leverage The use of a small amount of capital or equity in combination with a large amount of debt in order to achieve a higher yield not possible with use of the equity alone.

liabilities All claims against a company such as debts, dividends, salaries, taxes, accounts payable.

life of contract The first to the last trading day in a futures contract.

limit In commodities, the maximum price fluctuation permitted by the exchange from the previous session's settlement price. Separate limits are established by the individual exchanges for each commodity.

limit order An instruction to a broker for a purchase at a price not above a specified maximum, or a sale at a price not below a specified minimum.

liquidation The conversion of securities or property into cash. In commodities, it is a transaction that closes a former open position.

liquidity The facility with which a market can absorb the buying and selling of a security or commodity.

liquidity ratio *See* acid test ratio.

load A portion of the initial cost of shares in a mutual fund for transaction commissions and other expenses. There is usually no charge of this kind on redemption.

long or **long position** In securities, it means ownership. In options, it refers to options purchased. In commodities, it refers to the ownership of a futures contract or the ownership of the physical commodity.

long term When applied to capital gains, it refers to securities held for more than a year. For debt instruments, it refers to obligations of over one year.

lot A unit of trading such as a round lot or a job lot *(q.v.)*.

M Abbreviation used for 1,000; used to specify face value of bonds.

M1, M2, M3 Categories of the money supply. M1 consists of currency in the hands of the public, travelers checks, demand deposits (check book deposits), balances in NOW accounts, balances in accounts with automatic transfer services, and balances in credit union share draft accounts. M2 adds to M1 savings and small time deposits, some "repos," some Eurodollar deposits, and private shares in money market mutual funds. M3 adds to M1 and M2 large time deposits, some "repos," and institutional shares in money market mutual funds.

maintenance call Margin call *(q.v.)*.

margin The amount of collateral, in cash or securities, required to be on deposit in a brokerage account to maintain certain credit positions such as short sales. The amount varies depending on Federal Reserve regulations and on the size and number of positions current.

margin account A brokerage account in which the customer leaves the necessary margin on deposit to make use of credit from the broker. A margin account is necessary for short sales, most options, and all futures.

margin call A demand from a broker that the client deposit additional equity (cash or securities) into a margin account in order to meet Federal Reserve or brokerage requirements.

market The total facilities for buying or selling a security, including the anticipated supply and demand.

market maker Usually refers to brokers or dealers who actively purchase and sell a specific OTC security for their own accounts and who post their bid and asked prices in the NASDAQ computer system or in the pink sheets. In options and commodities, it is an exchange member who trades for his own account but who may be (one of several) assigned to specific securities or commodities.

market order *See* at-the-market.

market value The price at which a security can be publicly bought or sold at a given time on an exchange or over the counter.

marketable securities Securities that may readily be purchased or sold; sometimes used to mean securities for which there is an active secondary market.

maturity The day on which a bond is due for redemption. In commodities, it is the period during which delivery may be made.

merger A takeover that has the cooperation of the board of the target company.

minus tick *See* down tick.

monetary policy Refers to the management of the money supply, usually the domain of the Federal Reserve Bank.

money market funds A mutual fund that invests exclusively in short-term debt instruments. *See* mutual fund.

money market instrument Short-term debt such as Treasury bills and commercial paper. Usually purchased at discount (less than face value) and redeemed at par.

money supply   Usually defined by the categories M1, M2, or M3 *(q.v.),* although there are categories that go up to M5.

mortgage bond   A bond issue secured by all or part of the real assets of the company.

MSE   Midwest Stock Exchange; also the Montreal Stock Exchange.

multiple   *See* price/earnings ratio.

municipal bond   Debt obligations issued by states and their political subdivisions and by certain agencies and authorities within the state. Interest is exempt from federal income tax and from the taxes of some states.

mutual fund   An open-end investment company. An unlimited number of shares are sold, and the capital is invested in other companies. Mutual funds redeem their own shares. *See* money-market funds.

naked options   An option sold when the writer does not own the underlying stock or an offsetting option position.

NASD   *See* National Association of Securities Dealers.

NASDAQ   *See* National Association of Securities Dealers Automated Quotations.

National Association of Securities Dealers (NASD)   An association of brokers and dealers engaged in securities transactions in the United States. It is the regulatory body for all over-the-counter brokers and dealers and is supervised by the SEC.

National Association of Securities Dealers Automated Quotations (NASDAQ)   A nationwide computerized system for security dealers to post prices, record transactions, and effect security transactions for issues listed in the system. It is the major over-the-counter trading method. *See* National Quotation Service.

National Quotation Service (NOS)   Maintained by the National Quotation Bureau, it reports on OTC securities not quoted by the NASDAQ system. Pink sheets list OTC stocks, their market makers, and bid and asked prices. Yellow sheets contain reports on corporate bonds.

negotiable security   A security whose title is easily transferable, as on delivery.

net asset value (NAV)   For open-end investment companies (mutual funds and money market funds), it is the net worth of all securities held by the fund. Per share net asset value is that amount divided by the total number of shares outstanding. For other types of companies, it is the net worth of all assets.

net change   The difference between the current price, usually a closing price, and the closing price of the previous trading session.

net current assets   *See* working capital.

net earnings   *See* net income.

net income   Profit; income after deducting all expenses from revenues.

net profit   *See* net income.

net sales   An item on the balance sheet indicating the receipts from sales minus the cost of those sales.

net tangible asset value per share   Book value per share.

net worth   *See* shareholder's equity.

new issue   A security which is being offered for the first time. In the stock tables, such an issue is specified "n" for one year to indicate that the 52-week high and low are as of the inception of trading and not literally 52 weeks.

next day contract   A securities transaction requiring payment the following day.

no-load mutual fund   A mutual fund that does not have a sales charge.

nominal yield   Coupon rate.

noncompetitive bid   In the case of government securities, this is an application submitted from an individual for a new government issue (bond, note, or bill). The price of the instrument will be pegged at the average price paid by brokers submitting competitive bids. *See* competitive bids.

noncumulative preferred stock   Preferred stock whose omitted dividends are not cumulative.

nonmarketable securities   Securities difficult or impossible to sell. Sometimes used to mean securities for which there is no secondary market.

nonrecurring item   *See* extraordinary item.

notice day   Any day on and after which a notice of intent to deliver may be issued to the holder of a futures contract.

NQB   National Quotation Bureau, Inc.

NYSE   New York Stock Exchange.

OCC   Option Clearing Corporation.

odd lot   An amount of stock less than a round lot, which is usually 100 shares. Securities that do not trade actively are sometimes traded in

10-share lots and, on the AMEX, in 10-, 25-, and 50-share lots. In these cases, an odd lot is less than the round lot stipulated. In Canada, the term "broken lot" is used. For commodities trading, it is an amount more or less than the usual contract specification, also called a job lot.

odd-lot theory   A theory which states that peaks in odd-lot purchases precede a fall in the market. It is based on the belief that small investors (those that buy odd lots) must be wrong.

offset   The closing or liquidation of a futures position.

open contract   *See* open interest.

open-end investment company   *See* mutual fund.

open interest   The total number of option or futures contracts outstanding that have not been closed—or, in the case of commodities, liquidated or offset by delivery.

opening transaction   The initial buying or selling of an option contract.

operating margin   Also called the expense ratio or the operating ratio, this is the operating costs divided by the net sales.

option   A contract granting the right to buy (*see* call) or to sell (*see* put) a specified amount of securities at a fixed price for a designated amount of time. One may buy or one may sell (called *write*) either type of contract.

Option Clearing Corporation (OCC)   The corporation that processes all option transactions. After a transaction is completed between the buyer and seller (writer) on an exchange floor, the OCC interposes itself as seller for the buyer and buyer for the seller. In this way no link is maintained between the original parties in the transaction. The OCC then randomly assigns the exercises to parties in short positions as they are received from parties in long positions.

OTC   *See* over-the-counter.

out of the money   An option with no intrinsic value in terms of the relationship between the striking price and the current price of the underlying security.

overbought   A condition whereby a security is bid up by speculative buying beyond reasonable levels.

oversubscribed   The condition of a new issue when there have been more securities requested than there are available. When this happens, each subscription is reduced proportionally until the total equals the amount available. Such issues usually increase in value immediately upon issuance. In takeover bids, or offers to repurchase stock (by the original company), it is the condition whereby more shares are offered than originally requested. Share purchases may then be made on a pro rata basis or declined altogether.

over-the-counter (OTC)   The market for securities not listed on a national or regional exchange. Prices of the most active are available from NASDAQ and the less active on the pink sheets. Government and municipal bonds are OTC as well as the stocks of many banks and insurance companies.

paid-in capital   Amount the company received above par value from the sale of stock.

paper loss or **profit**   An unrealized loss or profit on a security that is still held and that would become real if the security were sold or the position closed.

par   (1) A value assigned to stock of a new issue for bookkeeping purposes. It has no relationship to intrinsic worth or market value of the stock, although it appears as a value on the balance sheet. (2) For preferred stock, it may be the dollar value on which the dividend percent is calculated. (3) For bonds, it is the face value on which the interest percent is calculated.

par value   *See* par.

partnership   Ownership of a business by two or more persons. Each partner shares in the direction of the company and in the liability for debt. *See* partnership, limited.

partnership, limited   A partnership with two kinds of partners. Limited partners share in ownership and financial liability, but general partners (often there is only one) make the business decisions. General partners are often other partnerships or corporations.

parity   An option trades at parity when the striking price plus the premium equal the current market price of the underlying security.

participating preferred stock   An issue of preferred stock that may yield, in addition to the stated dividend, additional dividends once expected common stock dividends have been paid.

PE   Philadelphia Stock Exchange

penny stock   Low-priced issues whose quotations are often stated in cents rather than in fractions of a point. Sometimes used to indicate any low-priced stock.

P/E ratio   *See* price/earnings ratio.

pink sheets   A quotations service for stocks not on an exchange and not listed by NASDAQ. The list, printed on pink paper, shows market makers and, usually, bid and asked prices. Such issues are not quoted in newspapers, but the pink sheets are distributed to brokerages daily.

pit   The trading areas of a futures exchange.

plus tick   *See* up tick.

point   For stock quotations it is $1; for bond quotations it is $10, assuming a par value of $1,000.

poison pill   An antitakeover measure adopted by the board of a target company designed to make the company less attractive to the acquirer.

portfolio   The total securities held by an investor or institution.

preferred stock   Stock with a fixed dividend rate. This dividend (which may be cumulative) must be paid before the dividend of any common stock. Preferred stockholders do not usually have voting privileges.

premium   (1) The price of an option. (2) The amount that the strike price and option price combined are above the current market price of the underlying security.

premium, trading at   When a bond is priced above the par value.

prepaid expenses   An item on the balance sheet that includes items like insurance and rent which are likely to be paid in advance.

price/earnings ratio   The number of times the per share price of the stock exceeds the per share earnings of the company.

price limit   The maximum amount the price of a futures contract can move from the settlement price of the previous period.

primary distribution   The initial sale of a new issue of securities. Distribution, through an investment banker, is usually over the counter. Also called *primary offering* or *initial distribution*.

primary earnings per share   *See* earnings per share.

primary market   The market for new issues. Sometimes used to mean the organized stock exchanges.

prime rate   The interest rate charged by a bank for loans to its most creditworthy customers.

principal   (1) Capital. (2) Face value of a bond. (3) The client for whom a securities transaction is made by a broker (as agent). When a brokerage buys and sells for its own account, it acts as principal.

principals   Stockholders.

private sector   That portion of the economy controlled by corporate, business, or individual spending, as opposed to the public sector.

privately held   Often used to mean the owning of a corporation by a handful of stockholders. Legally, it means the shares of a corporation that have never been offered publicly. Such a company is not subject to periodic reporting requirements.

profit taking   Selling stock for capital gain; often used to describe sales that follow (and sometimes halt) a short rally.

proprietorship   Ownership of a business by an individual. Individual has personal liability for debts of business.

proxy   In corporate business, the legal authority to exercise another shareholder's vote.

proxy contest   The attempt of a person or group of people to obtain the proxies of a sufficient number of shareholders to influence a corporate election or vote.

prudent man rule   A standard by which one invests with caution for reasonable income and preservation of capital.

PSE   Pacific Stock Exchange

public debt   government debt, whether federal or municipal.

public financing   Federal, state, or municipal financing.

public, go   For a company to issue stock, available to the public, for the first time. This is called an initial offering.

public offering   An offering of a large number of shares for sale to the general public, usually from the issuing company.

public sector   That portion of the economy controlled by federal, state, or local spending, as opposed to the private sector.

public utilities   Utility companies, whether publicly or privately owned.

publicly held   A corporation whose shares are held by a large number of shareholders. It is assumed that ownership of such shares is freely transferable.

put   An option giving the right to sell 100 shares (usually) of a specific stock, at a specific price, within a specific time period.

quick assets   Current assets minus the inventory.

quick asset ratio   *See* acid test ratio.

quotation or **quote**   In investing, a verbal or printed representation of a securities price. It may be a transaction price, or it may consist of both a bid and an asked price.

ratio strategy   Any number of option spreads and combinations in which the short positions exceed the long positions.

real capital   Consists of equipment, machinery, or buildings, used in production.

real estate investment trust (REIT)   A closed-end investment company that invests in real estate.

real GNP *See* gross national product.

recession A period in the economy marked by the reduction of production, sales, profits, employment, and sometimes prices. Not thought to be as severe as a depression.

record date *See* holder of record.

redemption price (1) For bonds, it is the price at which a bond will be redeemed should it be called before maturity. Often this is a figure above par value. (2) For mutual funds, it is the price at which shares can be redeemed, usually the net asset value.

red herring A preliminary prospectus (description) of a new issue being offered by an underwriter. The caveats must be printed in red on the first page.

registered as to interest only Bonds for which interest is sent automatically to the registered holder but for which face value is returned (at maturity) only to the bearer.

registered as to principal only A coupon bond which will return the face value (at maturity) automatically to the registered holder.

registered bond *See* fully registered bond.

registered representative An employee of a brokerage who has been trained and is registered to handle customer accounts. Also known as an *account executive*. Such an individual is not, strictly speaking, a broker.

Regulation T call A margin call.

rehypothecation A broker's practice of pledging customers' securities from their margin accounts in order that those securities may serve as collateral at a bank for the financing of a customer's debit balance in those accounts.

repo *See* repurchase agreement.

repurchase agreement A federal open market committee arrangement with a dealer in which the dealer contracts to purchase a government or agency security at a fixed price, with a provision for its resale at the same price at competitive interest rates.

reserve requirement A commercial bank's obligation to retain a specified percentage of its deposits in vault cash or in a non-interest-bearing account with a Federal Reserve bank.

retained earnings That part of the earnings of a company not distributed to the stockholders and kept by the corporation.

retirement of debt paying off the principal of a bond, loan, or debt instrument.

return *See* yield.

return on equity   The net income divided by the shareholders' equity.

return on invested capital   Net income and interest expenses divided by the total capitalization.

revenue anticipation note (RAN)   A short-term (one year or less) municipal note backed by anticipated revenues. Usually issued at discount in denominations of $25,000.

revenue bonds   Municipal bonds of several types which are backed by revenue from a special project tax.

reverse split   Division of the total number of shares outstanding to a lesser number. A ten for one reverse split would result in the shareholder owning 10 shares for every 100 formerly held. Frequently done to get the share price out of the range of penny stock *(q.v.)*.

right   Allows the holder to purchase additional shares at a stipulated price for a stipulated time period. *See* unit.

risk arbitrage   A kind of arbitrage usually associated with takeovers whereby the arbitrageur buys the stock of the target company and sells the stock of the company attempting the takeover. *See* arbitrage.

rollover   Reinvesting funds from a maturing security into longer-term securities. Applicable to debt instruments, options, and futures.

round lot   Standard unit of trading. For stocks, it is 100 shares except for some inactive issues traded in 10-share lots. On the AMEX there are also a few that trade in 25- and 50-share lots. For futures, the contract size is specified separately for each commodity on each exchange.

round trip   Both the opening transaction and closing transaction in a futures position. Commission in commodities is charged per roundtrip.

seasoned security   Either an equity or a debt instrument already in the hands of the public such that its sale would be between investors, not between the issuing company and an investor. *See* secondary market.

seat   A membership on an exchange.

SEC   *See* Securities and Exchange Commission.

secondary distribution   A public offering of a large block of stock held by the issuing company or one or more large stockholders at a time after the primary distribution. Also called *secondary offering. See* special offering.

secondary market   The trading of securities any time after their initial distribution. *See* aftermarket. Sometimes used to mean the trading of securities not listed on an exchange.

secondary offering   *See* secondary distribution.

securities Sometimes used to mean only stocks and bonds; in a broader sense includes almost any financial instrument. Sometimes implies a longer-term vehicle than, for example, "instrument."

Securities and Exchange Commission (SEC) The government agency that regulates the securities industry.

Securities Investor Protection Corporation A government-sponsored private corporation that insures securities accounts in brokerages up to $100,000 in the event of a brokerage bankruptcy or failure.

serial bond Bonds of the same issue but with different maturities and coupon rates.

settlement price The official closing price for a commodity set by the clearinghouse at the end of each trading day. This is the price from which margin requirements and price limits for the next day are calculated. The final transaction price is used whenever possible, but often there are a number of simultaneous trades in the closing moments of a session. When this happens, a price near the midpoint of the various transaction prices is selected.

shareholders' equity *See* book value.

shares *See* stock.

shelf distribution The right of an officer of a corporation or a holder of 10% or more of the stock to dispose of a sizable number of shares from his or her portfolio ("shelf") over a nine-month period following the effective date.

short or **short position** When one has made a short sale or when one has sold an option or a futures contract. *See* long.

short-against-the-box Selling a security short that one also owns (in the same quantity).

short covering A purchase on a securities or commodities market in order to close a short position or sale, or to return stock previously borrowed.

short interest Number of shares that have been sold short *(q.v.)* and not yet "covered"—that is, bought back and returned to the brokerage.

short interest ratio The total number of shares sold short (that haven't been covered yet) divided by the average daily trading volume for the reporting period. For the New York Stock Exchange the ratio does not usually get above 1.90, and higher is considered a bullish indicator.

short sale The sale of a security that is borrowed for this purpose from one's broker. It is necessary to have a margin account for this purpose. The expectation is that when the security is purchased at a later date, in order to repay the broker, the price will have gone down and the investor will realize the difference between the two prices as profit. A short sale can take place only on an up tick (rise in price) of at least ⅛ point.

sinking fund   Funds set aside by a corporation, usually annually, to retire outstanding bonds and sometimes preferred stock.

SIPC   *See* Securities Investor Protection Corporation.

specialist   A member of an exchange charged with maintaining an orderly market in one or more securities. To this end the specialist buys and sells for his own account as well as for others, often absorbing temporary disparities between supply and demand.

special offering   A secondary distribution (also called secondary offering) of securities from the issuing company in accordance with plans which the company has registered with the SEC. The plans must specify price, commission, and other terms of the offering.

speculator   An individual willing to assume higher risk in return for higher gain. In some trading situations, it is an individual willing to take the risks others are seeking to avoid. In commodities, it is an individual who trades in futures but does not intend to make or accept delivery.

split   A division of shares into, usually, a larger number. A 2 for 1 split would double the number of shares held by any investor, and each share would be worth half as much as before. Reverse splits are also possible.

spot commodity   *See* actuals.

spot market   *See* cash market.

spot price   Prices quoted for actuals or cash commodities.

spread   The difference between the bid and asked price of a security.

spread option   A strategy whereby one simultaneously buys one option and sells another on the same security in order to lock in a price or so that the gain on one will offset a loss on the other.

statement of changes in financial position   A section of the annual report showing increase or decrease in working capital.

statement of operations   *See* income statement.

statement of stockholders' equity   *See* changes in stockholder's equity.

stock   A unit of ownership in a corporation. There are two major types: common stock and preferred stock.

stock ahead   Refers to a situation where other orders for the same security are ahead of yours on the floor of the exchange. This can result in a price change by the time your order can be executed.

stock exchange An institution that provides the facilities for the trading of stocks, bonds, warrants, options, and sometimes other securities. The exchanges themselves do not purchase, sell, or set prices for securities. Trading is done by or through members of the exchange, and the securities must be registered on that exchange.

stock index future A futures contract based on a stock index. Index numbers are assigned a monetary value and settlement is in cash.

stock split *See* split.

stockholder of record Any party whose name as a shareholder is recorded on the books of the issuing company.

stockholders' equity Difference between assets and liabilities. On the balance sheet, the stockholders' equity usually includes the par value of preferred stock, the par value of common stock, the paid-in capital, and the retained capital.

straddle An option strategy involving a put and a call on the same underlying security. In commodities, it is a spread in futures other than grains.

strap options An option strategy involving one put and two calls on the same underlying security.

street name Indicates that securities are being held for the purchaser by a brokerage.

strike price *See* exercise price.

subordinated debt instrument A bond whose claim to the assets of a corporation, or whose repayment of principal, is subordinated to another debt instrument.

subscription privilege Right of present shareholders to obtain a proportion of a new offering from the same company that is in proportion to their present holding. Often shares so obtained are below the market price.

support A term from technical analysis indicating a price area where buyer demand is expected to keep the price of a security from falling through a specific level.

TAN *See* tax anticipation note.

takeover Acquisition of enough shares in a company to control it. If takeover is with the cooperation of the board of the target company, it is usually referred to as a *merger*.

target company Company that another company or individual is trying to take over.

tax anticipation note (TAN) A short-term (one year or less) municipal note backed by anticipated proceeds from a forthcoming tax collection. Usually issued at discount in denominations of $25,000.

tax bracket The percent of federal taxes you pay. Note that for calculating yield from tax-exempt bonds, you should use the tax bracket you *would be in* if you received the contemplated amount from a taxable source.

tax-exempt securities *See* municipal bond.

tax-free bond *See* municipal bond.

tax shelter An investment by means of which certain costs can be deducted from taxable income, or from which income is tax-exempt.

technical analysis An approach to investing based on the examination of the previous price movements of a security. Usually thought of in contrast to fundamental analysis.

technical rally A brief upturn in security prices caused by factors other than a fundamental shift in the supply and demand for that security. It is not expected to reverse the prevailing downward trend.

10K A no-frills annual report required by and filed with the SEC by all corporations in the United States except those that are closely held (*q.v.*).

tender offer Large-scale public offers to buy shares of a particular stock, sometimes with the intention of taking control of a corporation. The buyer may reserve the right to decline, at a later date, all or a part of the shares subsequently presented.

term bond A bond issue consisting of bonds that mature on the same date and have the same coupon rate. *See* serial bond. Also, a Treasury bond that can be called before maturity.

thin market Lack of trading activity for a specific security, commodity, or an entire market. Prices are somewhat more volatile under these conditions.

third market Over-the-counter trading by brokerages of securities that are listed on an exchange.

tick The minimum price fluctuation for a futures contract. The amount is specified separately for each commodity by each exchange.

ticker Quotations that are trade-by-trade transaction reports which specify the name, price, and usually the volume of each stock, warrant, bond, option, or commodity traded on an exchange. *See* consolidated tape.

time spread *See* calendar spread.

time value premium The amount of an option's premium above its intrinsic value. This is the value which declines with time.

tombstone A newspaper ad for a new issue, called "tombstone" for the traditional black border and heavy print.

total capitalization or **long-term capitalization** Total assets minus intangible assets and current assets.

Treasury securities Direct debt obligations of the U.S. government issued in bills, bonds, and notes.

treasury stock Issued stock that has been required by a corporation. It is still counted as issued stock, but not *issued and outstanding*.

TSE Toronto Stock Exchange.

type Used in option trading to distinguish puts and calls. Options of one type would either be all calls or all puts.

uncovered option *See* naked option.

unit New issues are sometimes initially offered in units, each of which may consist of one or more shares of stock and one or more warrants.

underwriter *See* investment banker.

up tick A transaction at a price greater than the previous one. Also called a plus tick.

venture capital Money available for investment in new or undeveloped companies.

vertical spread An option strategy consisting of the simultaneous purchase and sale of puts or of calls with the same expiration date and different exercise prices.

volume The number of shares or contracts traded.

voting trust The deposit of stock with a trustee, usually a commercial bank, by stockholders for the purpose of eventually gaining control of a corporation. Stockholders receive a voting trust certificate in return for their stock.

warrant A certificate granting the long-term privilege (5 to 10 years) of purchasing more shares of stock from a company at a specified price. Warrants may be traded like stock.

when distributed A security trading in advance of the printing of the certificate.

when issued A security trading in advance of its final authorization for issuance. Should the security not be authorized, all trades will be canceled.

white knight   A company considered desirable as an acquiring company in lieu of another company considered undesirable.

"Whoops" bonds   Bonds issued by the Washington (State) Public Power Supply System to finance the construction of nuclear power plants.

working capital   Current assets minus current liabilities. Roughly, this is the amount of money the company has to operate with for the fiscal year.

working capital ratio   *See* current ratio.

World Bank   *See* International Bank for Reconstruction and Development.

write   To sell an option.

yield   Dividends or interest from a security, expressed as a percent of purchase price or of par. *See* yield to maturity.

yield to maturity   An annualized yield percent that takes into account the current yield, capital gain or loss at maturity, and reinvestment of all interest payments at the coupon rate.

zero-coupon bond   Type of bond that does not pay interest until maturity. It is sold at deep discount and redeemed, upon maturity, at face value (the face value includes the accrued interest). Taxes, however, must be paid each year on the nonpaid interest.

Index